EDINBURGH REV[...]

CONTENTS

**Edinburgh Review, 22 George Square
Edinburgh EH8 9LF**
tel 031-650 4689
fax 031-662 0053
editor   Murdo Macdonald
co-editor   Peter Kravitz
encyclopaedia editor   Ed Baxter
cover   Ann Ross Paterson
production   Pam O'Connor
publicity   Kathryn MacLean
logo   Alasdair Gray
c   the contributors

subscription   £16 for 4 issues
ISSN 0267 6672   ISBN 0 7486 6110 7

distributed in the UK by Edinburgh University Press
typeset in Sabon by Koinonia Ltd, Bury
printed by J.W.Arrowsmith, Bristol

Subsidised by The Scottish Arts Council

The editor regrets that the return of
unsolicited material cannot be guaranteed.

BY WAY OF AN EDITORIAL

Statement by Cildo Meireles   Glasgow   7 September 1990

1. Invited to make a project in Glasgow by TSWA, I made a proposal for a suggested site, the space between the two arches on John Street between the City Chambers and the Burgh Court.

I proposed to build a council house in this space.The project was concerned with the idea of centre and periphery, and with the idea of unity and multiplicity.

2. A few weeks before the project was due to be constructed, I was informed that Glasgow District Council had refused permission for its realisation. They did not explain why.

3. As I knew their refusal was not motivated by aesthetic reasons, nor by economic ones (TSWA had committed sufficient funds to complete the work), I then proposed a revised project.

A very small model of the council house was to be suspended on a golden string. Its installation would cause no damage to the adjacent buildings. It would cause no obstruction to traffic or pedestrians; it presented no technical problems.

At the same time, I suggested another site for the second project.

The City Council refused both proposals. Again they did not explain why.

4. So - It was not refused for aesthetic reasons.

It was not refused for budgetary reasons.

It was not refused for technical reasons.

It was refused for some other obscure reason. The function of a work of art is to shed some light on this kind of obscurity, to try and talk through this conspiracy of silence.

5. I myself consider that censoring the word censorship is the strange way Glasgow District Council found to celebrate the freedom of expression in the Cultural Capital of Europe 1990.

Cildo Meireles

After the Jamboree: THE RECKONING.

Glasgow's great Year of Culture had more to do with power politics than culture, more to do with millionaire developers than art.

But a debate was opened up and sustained throughout the year which the Labour Council, the festivals unit, the property speculators and entrepreneurs could well have done without.

Here, in The Reckoning, the argument continues. Biting insights into the secret agenda of the 'New Glasgow' are combined with fiction inspired by this great city.

Once again the real Glasgow stands up.

Edited by Farquhar McLay
with
Donald Anderson * Freddy Anderson * Norman Bissell *
John Taylor Caldwell * Ned Donaldson * Michael Donnelly
* William Gilfedder * Alasdair Gray * James Kelman *
Robert Lynn * J.E. MacInness * Ian McKechnie
* Brendan McLaughlin * J.N. Reilly * Hugh Savage *
Jeff Torrington * Jack Withers * James D. Young

Clydeside Press

Price: £3.95

WORK

BRIDGET PENNEY

CARLOS ALVAREZ

DAVID MACKENZIE

Incidents on the Road

Bridget Penney

Police block.

It was as if I'd been exposed to an electric shock. All the revulsion I'd felt for my job over the past months welled up at once, and I started to walk towards the door, past the whining machines beneath the bright light and the figures bowed above them, transfixed by the continual rattle of coins.

– Where are going, Judy?

– Piss off.

She flushed and stepped across me to bar my way. I stood there, mute, and glowered at her. She regained her calm, and spoke steadily

– Not with those things.

My fingers seemed very large as I fumbled with the knots that held the overall in place. Her face was still. As knots unravelled, the rolls of money dug into my stomach. I pulled the garment over my head and used my arm as a spindle, closing the money within a tight roll of cloth in a gesture that became increasingly futile as I sensed the smile spreading across her face.

– Judy.

I tossed the roll at the ground where it struck her ankle, and brushed past out into the salt air, following the line of the wooden planks until I'd quit the pier and was heading along the esplanade, between the sea and the afternoon traffic. It was hot, and I began to sweat. As I slowed, the wind off the sea caught me, and my clothes felt like ice.

A car pulled up. I glanced at it involuntarily and caught the eye of the woman leaning across as if to ask me directions.

Her eyes were watery and bloodshot. She had reddish hair and pale skin that looked firm and healthy. I found myself saying

– I'll show you

and saw her hand move to unlock the door, smiling as I opened it and slipped inside.

– This is very kind of you, she said as the car pulled away from the kerb. I wriggled slightly in my seat. The overheated upholstery threatened to stick to the back of my legs.

– Can you put on the belt, she said, taking one hand from the wheel to indicate it – in case we get stopped.

I bent forward, and stole a glance up at her. A private smile played around her lips, which were pale and dry, giving the impression they had not enough skin. Her chin was sharp, but blurred by a suggestion of fat.

– There are some cigarettes in there.

I took the hint, lit one, and passed it over. She held it gingerly, inhaled deeply, and coughed. Then she opened the window and threw it out. I found a packet of pastilles in the glove compartment and passed her one. She sucked noisily for a second, then spat it out.

– Thanks, she said. Her cough had gone.

She changed gears as we turned off the coast road and headed uphill. I leaned back in my seat: the cold wind ventilating the car made it quite pleasant. I smoothed my clothes and undid the top button of my blouse, scraped my hair up from my neck and let it fan out over the back of the seat. Then I teased off one shoe with the toe of the other, rotating my heel to study the clinging patch where a blister had burst against the dark nylon.

– Why don't you take your gloves off?

I laughed out loud and glanced down at my hands encased in black cotton. Looking up again, I caught her eye. She shook her head and smiled a bit, then turned away.

– It was part of my job, I said, fumbling with words for what already seemed remote. Staring down at my hands as if I couldn't quite believe them, I laughed again, rather oddly.

– What was your job.

– Changing people's money in the arcade so they could put it in machines.

– Sounds terrible.

I gestured self-consciously. Without removing her eyes from the road she gave me another quick smile, and pulled across into a different lane. Idly I raised my hands, then lowered them.

There was activity up ahead. The traffic had come to a halt, and there were lights across the road, blinking ineffectually against the glare of the sun setting over in the west. They cast weak shadows upwards, elongating the trees at the side of the road so they threatened to close over. I rolled down the window and stuck out my head to look along the column of cars. There was a restless movement next to me as she drummed at the steering wheel with her fingers.

– There's a man coming. A policeman.

She raised her shoulders indifferently and sighed.

– There must have been an accident.

He went to her side of the car, asked for her licence. She handed it over with a flippant gesture. He straightened up, and studied it for some time before passing it back.

– What's wrong with it?

His face showed that he resented her tone. He glanced from her to the car and back.

– There's been a murder.

It barely showed but he succeeded in rattling her.

– Two young women had their throats cut in the North Wood.

– That's the other side of town, I interposed, leaning across her.

– Why are you stopping people here?

– We've got men on all the roads.

As I stared up at him for a moment his face worked. Then he turned and marched back along the column, his shadow brushing up against the cars.

– You alright, I said to the woman. She shrugged impatiently. I put my gloved hand on hers where it rested on the wheel, lightly touching all her fingers. After a second she removed it and didn't look at me.

The policeman returned with another, older man. I could see them arguing as they came along.

– Sorry to bother you girls.

She passed a hand across her forehead.

– What's the matter, officer?

He gave her a warily sympathetic look, then glanced at his colleague, who stubbornly resisted the glance and addressed himself to us.

– Someone described a car like yours parked near the wood.

The woman raised her head and spoke scathingly.

– You mean someone said they saw a black car. There are hundreds.

He looked as if he might have shrugged.

– It was a specific description.

There was a moment of silence.

– Are you going to arrest me, she said softly.

Her eyes flickered from one to the other. I stirred in my seat, disconcerted by the directness of her challenge.

The older man cleared his throat.

– Perhaps you can tell us something.

– We came down from London this morning.

I glanced aside as if for corroboration. – We were going to drive along the coast, then find somewhere to stay.

– What's your name?

– Judy Smith.

He gave me a tired smile.
- Alright girls. We shouldn't keep you much longer.
Then I watched him walk to the head of the column. The younger man had gone to check on the cars behind us.
She sighed and scratched her head.
- I don't like the police.
It was practically dark in the car, and the shadowed outline of her face made me feel somehow peaceful. I let myself stretch out as far as the seat allowed. A gratifying, almost titillating exhaustion spread through my limbs.
- What's your name, I said on the verge of a yawn.
- Laura.

River.
We drove for most of the night. Slight changes in the engine's pitch made me aware, in my semi-conscious state, where the road varied. Sometimes I raised myself to look as a white wall flashed by.
   Just before dawn we pulled onto a rough track, then slithered across grass. Something brushed the roof of the car as we came to a halt.
   I must have slept again for when I woke it was light. Laura was doing something at the front of the car. For a moment I lay still, eyes half closed, to listen to the faint sounds she made. Then I tentatively stretched my neck, and one by one my limbs, until cramp receded and I opened the door and got out.
   We were parked underneath a tree. On either side the boughs bent down gently to cloak us, creating a barrier of leaves through which the diffused light shone green. I walked to the edge of the circle and ran my arms up along the branches until a satisfying coolness drenched my clothes and the scent of the leaves made me giddy.
- Feel better?
I turned. She was standing behind me. There was a smear of oil on her left cheek and her eyes were barely open.
- You should have woken me if you wanted help.
She smiled and shook her head.
- You must have been tireder than I was.
Her tone was friendly, but there existed a slight reserve which might have been due to tiredness. I stepped back a little and made a sort of self-conscious gesture round about.
- Why here?
She shrugged.
- I don't like to park near the road. You get people coming along.
- How did you find your way in the dark?

She gave me a guarded smile and said
– You don't have to bother about that Judy.

She turned quickly, leaving me at a loss, and walked back to the car, her light shoes making little sound. The green shadows gave everything an eerie tint. Slowly I rolled up my wet sleeves. My forearms glowed as I parted the curtain of leaves and stepped outside. We were on a riverbank. The sun was still low in the sky but the last traces of mist were already dispelling. My feet sank into sodden grass. I tried to gauge the time from the sun's position and let my failure yield to a sense of pleasant aimlessness. Any noises I could hear were much too faint to provide a clue.

I studied my surroundings with passive deliberation, gaining such satisfaction from the way I moved that I felt the desire to do something extravagant fill me with a slow excitement that was hard to contain. The field behind me was empty, the road invisible.

On the opposite bank rushes grew close to the water. I stared at the coal black mud, castellated by the river's progress. Its current was hard to discern: just a few faint ripples indicated a tug towards the far bank. My head turned to look along. A flat stretch of grey, running straight where the bank had been improved. Then a smudge of trees, and it vanished, curving slowly beyond my sight.

Taking off my stained clothes, I slipped into the cold water. First shock expelled the air from my lungs, then I kicked out strongly, loving the feeling of moving through water the sun had not yet begun to warm, enjoying the silky texture that suggested it would be unbearable later in the day. I hadn't felt so good in a long time. My legs and arms pumped through the water in perfect tune.

– Oh Laura this is marvellous come in.

She was standing on the bank with her arms crossed, watching me. Her presence made my satisfaction a little more deliberate. I kicked out my legs in a mighty splash, conscious of a desire to tease her, and saw her flinch as a few drops of water fell dangerously near in the sunlight.

– I'll teach you to swim, I persisted, generous in the sense of the advantage.

As she shook her head the sun caught her face and the furrow between her brows.

– I think you can drown enough for both of us.

I laughed. As I heaved round on my stomach to tread water her expression evolved into a complexity that puzzled me.

– Let's get on our way. Can you drive.

I nodded. As I climbed up the bank she looked at me with a glance that mingled amusement and something else.

– Where are we going?

She made a casual gesture. – I've got some stuff stored in a place a few miles from here.

– And then?

I was drying my feet with overdirected care. As I straightened up it was as if her eyes had moved away from me rather sharply.

– Oh.

Her manner was offhand. – Anywhere you like.

I donned my clothes soberly, feeling slightly ashamed of playing her up. As I walked with her back to the car her expression was warm but brittle. She was more nervous than I had suspected or perhaps tiredness exaggerated her reactions.

I really liked her. She was tricky, which I appreciated, and made me less worried about being moody myself. She had a car, and wherever I might end up it was better than stewing on the pier all summer.

House.

It was a long time since I had handled a car, and I experienced a steady, if rather remote, excitement as the road smoothly disappeared before me. Laura dozed in the passenger seat, her chin pressed right down against her neck. Occasionally a stifled snore escaped her. When this happened, I would glance across, and moving my eyes back, would catch an almost conspiratorial look in the mirror. Her hands lay limply in her lap. A slight swell of fat at the wrist was swiftly contained by buttoned cuffs which had that shiny look clothes get when they've been worn too long.

Her eyes opened with difficulty and she sat up.

– What is it? she said, seeing me grin.

– You, I said truthfully.

She wasn't quite sure she liked that.

– What about me?

I smiled and shook my head, devoting exaggerated care to the tension of the wheel between my hands.

We turned down a lane that rapidly petered out into a track. I had a dim glimpse of a pond, overhung by trees, and then Laura put her hand on the wheel. I braked a little too quickly and turned to her. She smiled.

– Do you want to come?

– Your stuff's here?

She raised her eyebrows and slipped out of the car. She walked with a slightly floundering motion, dipping and jerking to avoid the thick deposits of mud that lingered though there'd been no rain for a week. Mosquitoes and flies swarmed around us; I kept my hand up in front of my face to swat them away.

We came level with a broken paling. She stopped.
- Here? I echoed.
She bent her shoulder to lift a gate which hadn't been disturbed for a while. I followed her through onto a path that led up to a house of incredible decrepitude.
- I used to live here, she said, as if needing to explain.
It was alright inside, which worried me, because I felt that when it started to crumble it would do so very quickly. I followed her through the rooms, fitting my footsteps to her own in the obscure hope of minimizing disturbance.
- I was here as a child, she said. - My parents moved to London when I was eight.
- I would have been relieved.
A sideways smile suggested my desire to leave had reinforced her need to talk. She went on apologetically.
- I hated moving. As soon as we got to London my cat ran away.
For a moment she fidgetted uneasily.
- I'm sure she came back here. I wanted to come and look but they wouldn't let me.
Her voice went very small. I gingerly avoided leaning back against a door.
- It was only a cat Laura, I said, trying to comfort without sympathy.
Silence ensued. A nervous desire to laugh was tempered by vague horror as I stood there looking at her in the almost ruined house.
At last she sighed very quietly and said
- My stuff's in here.
Two suitcases and a grip, which she wiped casually before handing me the larger case. Without further words we left the house. I wasn't tempted to look back and don't know whether she was.

Café.
We were sitting together in a cafe drinking ice-cream sodas. Being Saturday morning, it was full of prospective teenage couples who made me self-conscious. Laura, who was either oblivious or better at concealing her reactions than I was, was gurgling with her straw at the last pink fragments that clung to the bottom of her glass. After a couple of sips at mine, I stirred it aimlessly, wishing I'd held out for a cup of coffee. I was impatient for Laura to finish but as she showed no signs of hurrying I picked up a paper a previous customer had left to make a pretence of reading it.
- Look, I said to Laura - about those girls who were killed.
I folded the paper appropriately and passed it across. A slight

frown creased her brows as she read, then shoved it back to me.
– So they caught someone.
– Seems so.
She shrugged. – Can I have your soda.
I passed it across without a word, watched with amusement as she
meticulously replaced my straw with her own.
– I keep expecting you to say you used to come here when you were
fourteen.
– Oh but I did, she said, in such a way that I was unable to tell
whether she was joking.
I plaited my fingers together on the table and leaned forward.
– Do you often revisit your past?
She sucked appreciatively at the straw.
– Judy, she said with great solemnity – it's in your honour.
We looked at each other, and simultaneously faltered. Her tone
was so close to mockery that for a moment we both doubted whether
it was. She cast down her eyes and fiddled with her glass, but her
composure was gone. I craned round the room with so visible a start
that I found it hard to believe we hadn't both become instantly
noticeable.
– I do like you, Judy, came from just above the glass.
I hardly dared reply or look at her.
– In all sorts of ways.
This time she looked up and met me with a disturbing smile. I found
something very sweet in her voice and was conscious of a desire to
prolong all the implications of that moment.
If this showed on my face it made her laugh.
– Judy, she said – let's go.
She pushed some coins beneath her saucer and abstracted the two
straws with a sleight of hand I was expected to see. Then another
smile, kinder because less challenging, and possessed of a gravity I'd
have found it hard to assume.
– Judy, she said again.
In some obscure way I'd already lost out. A flicker of concern
across her face betrayed the panic I'd let show in mine.
– Laura, I …
It was all bewilderingly clear. There was an injection of tenderness
into her smile. I passed out of the cafe with the strongest commitment
to something I knew nothing about.

The Bridge.
We went into a shop to buy provisions for our journey. Laura selected
biscuits and several cartons of fruit juice. While I half-heartedly

added a loaf, Laura took jam and a sheaf of chocolate bars. She paid
with a large note and I found myself carrying the bags. Laura walked
slightly ahead, whistling thoughtfully and twirling the bunch of keys
round one finger.

– It's too hot to drive now, she called back at me. – What do you
say we dump this stuff in the car and set off this evening.

She gave me a slightly teasing smile as if to indicate what a good
idea this was. I smiled agreement – it was her car, after all.

We reached the entrance of the underground carpark and descended.
There were narrow concrete steps at one side for pedestrians, but
Laura ignored them in favour of the ramps the cars went down,
seeming careless of any danger we might incur. She took the bag from
me and swung it as she walked with a slight swagger down the middle
of each slope through the chilly petrol-saturated gloom.

We put the stuff in the back, beside her luggage. As she was locking
up, I was taken by a feeling of awkwardness, half sad and half
reckless, as if I didn't really know what to do but was being overtaken
by events against my will. Staring at her back outlined by the coat in
the flickering light I had a confused impulse towards her, in which an
almost violent tenderness was dominated by something else that
made no sense to me. Turning, she smiled at me thoughtfully, and
taking my arm led me up the pedestrian steps into the sunlight.

– What would you like, Judy?

– Somewhere quiet.

She rubbed her free hand across her face as if tired or trying to
think. For some reason this aroused my suspicion, and I gave her a
quick mulish glare which she evaded, seeming about to say something
sharp, then changing her mind.

– I don't really know my way round here.

– Neither do I.

We looked at each other, then smiled.

– Let's wander.

She took my hand and squeezed it lightly. I looked down on her
fingers which were white and slightly plump. We both seemed to have
recovered our good humour. As we walked along, we responded to
a sense of complicity which took the form of throwing a mystery
round ourselves, emphasising our behaviour in peculiar ways and
engineering a private joke that permitted us to laugh at everything
around us. We covered the main streets in this way, but when we came
into the quieter suburbs we were more subdued, and strolled in
silence along the tree-lined streets, occasionally glancing at each
other, but mostly self-contained, soaking up the dull warmth of the
afternoon.

– Look Laura, I said suddenly – there's a bridge.

It poked up a little oddly behind the houses. She gave me a look as if she was trying not to laugh at me. I grew self-conscious, and stopped.

– Come on, she said – let's look at your old bridge.

It was at the end of the street. She took my arm again and led me on. She seemed amused with the whole thing. I didn't like her being amused with me, but thought if I demurred, it would be worse.

We climbed a flight of iron steps, then lolled against the sides of the walkway that spanned the tracks and platforms of a station. She peered over the edge, and I looked at her. As a train pulled in underneath she raised herself on her toes with a slight exclamation of surprise.

– It's hot, Judy.

I made my face as nonchalant as I could manage and she gave me a look perhaps intended for mystification. I found myself following her across the bridge, listening to the slightly mannered taps her shoes gave out against the iron.

At the bottom of the steps a narrow lane ran straight along beside a high wall. From the bridge I'd glimpsed trees, but when we found the gate and entered, it was a graveyard.

– Put on your gloves, Judy, Laura murmured. – And be a young widow, I'll support you.

Accordingly we proceeded. The place was overgrown, with the thick foliage of early summer already wilted by the scorching heat. But the paths had been freshly cleared, so the clipped back bushes presented a vivid uniform wall of green, and the impression was rather that of a well-maintained maze, than a cemetery. It was a place for assignations: every turn suggested a glimpse of someone slipping out of sight.

We passed slowly among obelisks and angels. The masquerade added a curious potency to our progress. Laura held me tightly, she stroked my hair and I buried my face in her shoulder. She was laughing very softly, right down in her chest, which I could hear because my head was pressed so close. Her heart beat slightly fast, and the sense of it pumping round all this warmth that surrounded me put a choke in my throat and an urgency in my grasp from which Laura wordlessly disengaged herself, pulling me to one side of the path where the leaves partially covered us.

She seemed to swallow before she spoke.

– Two kinds of people haunt cemeteries, she said. Her tone was light and dry but her eyes were anxious. – Ghouls and lovers. Which are you?

It was as if I was a stranger. Her eyes seemed to search my face over and over rapidly but reach no conclusion.

– A widow, I replied, falling in with her formal banter, and touched her hand.

– Why then you're both, she said in a tone at once grave and playful.

She turned my hand palm upward and seemed to study it for a moment, then stared at me slightly embarrassed. I kept my eyes steady and did not betray the strange focus of emotion within me. Then she looked aside, abruptly, and gave a sort of half smile to distract us both.

– What a place for it, she said, almost under her breath.

She made as if to step onto the path but I caught her hand and held her, determined to take the initiative for once.

– Judy, she said, and there was both alarm and annoyance in her tone.

– I love you, I said stubbornly. I could repeat it without looking at her and did, trying to get some sense into the words so she could see what I was at.

– Not here, Judy, she said.

Her face registered bafflement and panic.

– There are other places, but not here.

I let her bring me out onto the path. Then I looked up and said with great calmness

– I don't respect the dead.

She looked as if she didn't quite understand me.

– You don't respect them, she said as if making it clear for herself.

– Perhaps you should.

Hotel.

We were in the foyer of a cheap hotel. Laura was talking to the clerk while I stood by the stairs, gazing up at the short honey-coloured twisted pillars of wood that formed the bannisters gradually rising from sight. We had been driving all day, and I was stiff and sweaty from long confinement in the car.

Laura came over.

– Third floor, at the front.

– Sea view, I suggested, beginning to climb the stairs.

– If you look far enough over the roofs.

She sounded tired. I felt a twinge of guilt, moulded into protective compassion. I took one of her bags. My own was very light for there was little in it.

At the top of the shaft a smeared pane admitted the late glow of the sun. Our door was painted white. Once inside, I wedged the window open at the top and pulled the curtains across.

Laura was taking off her shoes.

– Are you hungry? I said on a curious impulse.

– No, Are you?

She looked at me straight for the first time in a while. For a moment I hesitated then smiled and shook my head. I got rather a tight smile in exchange.

– I'm going to sleep, she said and curled up under the coverlet.

I slipped through to the bathroom, ran the tub full of water, and soaked in it for a long while, topping up when it threatened to cool. No sound came from the adjacent room. It was dark when I emerged, so I cut the light before opening the door. A faint draught moved the top of the curtain, outlined by a whitish glow that seemed unnervingly precise.

It was some time before I realised I wasn't watching it alone. Then I was careful not to betray my knowledge, relishing the community that shared object gave us. So I was still. And then she turned, and looked at me.

– Couldn't sleep?

– Bad dreams.

I went to sit with her. She sighed, moving up in the bed, then rose abruptly and went to stand by the window. I followed her with my eyes, then looked down, conscious of something I could not account for.

– It's cold there Laura. Come back into bed where it's warm.

She shook her head, I resolved to watch her, then realised with a start that I'd been asleep for a while.

It had been raining for hours. The window was open and she was leaning there, deep in thought, with her chin in her hands.

This story comes from the collection *Honeymoon with Death and other stories* published by Polygon, spring 1991.

Carlos Alvarez
Six Poems

INTRODUCED AND TRANSLATED BY

David Johnston

DURING THE DARK years of Francoism, Carlos Alvarez (Jerez de la Frontera, 1933) was arguably Spain's most censored writer, with books published in Denmark, Sweden, Russia, France and Italy (as well as having received the Danish Lovemanken Prize and being proposed for the Nobel) before his first book even saw the light of day in his own native land. He first came to poetry in 1960 after his first period of imprisonment for 'anti-fascist activities', inspired by the understandable desire to speak out without fear of further reprisal. In his own words: 'I was a later starter. I wrote my first poem when I was 26 because of a biting need to express my opinions – fundamentally political opinions – in a way that would keep me out of prison. What couldn't be said in prose – and especially not in the press – might be said in the relatively coded language of poetry'. Alvarez's poetry is thus born from an historical sense deep within the bones that words matter, that ideas can be dangerous. 'No matter what you say, say nothing' was Seamus Heaney's not so ironical echoing of the Irish canniness rooted in the same sense, and in a similar way Carlos Alvarez came to clothe his protest in half-words and extended metaphor. 'I could never have been a pamphleteer anyway. A bourgeois education with its encumbent literary sensibility had knocked that on the head'. Of course, there was more to it than that. Like Howard Barker, who in 1986 advocated opposing the official philistinism of Thatcherism with the elaborated forms of high tragedy, Alvarez and others chose to confront regime-sponsored cultural mediocrity with a product of quality, a literature that restored to the individual his or her right to subjectivity, the right to the forbidden feelings of pain and loss.

It has often been said that the mark of good poetry is its ability to linger fresh in the memory. Usually it is little more than a piece of public breast-beating for the translator to insist on the poetic qualities of the original lines, but in the case of Carlos Alvarez his acknowledged mastery of rhythm and form, of the well-turned line, also has an important anecdotal significance. '27th September', for example, was written in solitary confinement during his fourth and final period of imprisonment when the sonnet form, with its strict rhyme and metre, was an aide-memoire in the attempt to use 'the pencil of imagination on the paper of memory'. But above all the poem possesses an important testimonial value in its denunciation of the execution of five young Basques on 27th September 1975 on the personal orders of General Franco, issued literally from his own death bed. Even so, at the heart of the poem there is still a human voice, not a political megaphone, because it is the poet's own sense of grief and loss which emerges from that of a nation (and, at the time, the whole international community) sunk in horror and, in the case of Spain at least, forcibly shrouded in silence.

As with Pablo Neruda, who at times felt *inescapably* Chilean, Alvarez's poetry is full of images of the nightmare of national history, a nightmare from which, unlike Stephen Dedalus, he refuses to try to waken. His best book is *Howl of the Wolfman*, a poetic investigation of the wholly accidental circumstances under which the poet is turned into a criminal under the full moon of oppression, just as Lawrence Talbot, in the original film, is horrified to find himself transformed into a monster. The circumstances may well be accidental, but only rarely do Alvarez's poems ignore the specific co-ordinates of time and space. 'Theory of Andalusia' takes the tourist map of flamenco Spain and turns it into a picture of human pain. 'A tale of two cities' is an evocation of two Spains, pre- and post-war, as radically different as Spanish Andalusia and rain-capped Gibraltar, under whose shadow the young Alvarez literally grew up. '24th July' is the monument to a moment's horror, the execution of the poet's father, a left-wing infantry captain, at the hands of the Nationalist authorities in Seville just as the Civil War was flaring.

Times, of course, are now easier in Spain, but Alvarez is quick to express his disillusion. 'The infrastructures are still the same. The only thing which has really changed is the right to freedom of speech. Just a few years ago in the new democracy I was able to accuse the Minister of the Interior publicly of complicity in the murder by the police of four young suspects. And nothing happened to me. There again, nothing happened to the policemen involved or to the Minister of the Interior either'. In this context, the final and most recent poem 'Another history lesson' reminds a society, indeed an entire civilisation, that forgetting is another form of fascism, that the lessons of the past must be remembered if its mistakes are not to be repeated.

*   *   *

24th JULY

Seville, 24th July 1936
Cáceres Prison, July 1965

My father who art in the earth
sown under July sun with your death
on an early morning of silence and lead ...
a saddened recollection of your likeness
gleaned from intuition;
from the lost fragments of a story
told to a child; from the clumsy gaze
of old family photographs,
which can only lie as they tell
of that day solemnly empty and in vain.
Because I have searched for you on many nights,
and with an artist's hands moulding the shapeless form
I have given private form to my imaginings
of the man who was José Alvarez,
so alike and so different from other men
in that part of his being that no longer breathes;
and different from me like the distant trunk
from the green branch, and yet where the same life flows ...
And in the workshop of my imagination
with the chisel of a grief contained
on the hard stone of a man shot and shot again
under the ripening sun, the brilliant laughing day,
you come to me in the only way I know,
through the startled sense of the barrier of the last few hours
crumbling to the void.
Your last night of passion lies heavy upon my nights,
and your grey dawn has weighed silently on mine
ever since the world has been world for me to touch,
since I began to question the silence of the things
that surround me, and that sometimes speak.
There were times I wanted to tell you
that I had tried to forget,
tried to cleanse the red stain
on family papers, the album, the ration book ...
and so many times I thought that I had,
that my fingers, rubbed raw,
would once again grow stiff and hard.
But, father, the truth is that those
who stained that book I tried to keep so clean

won't permit the waters to return to their source ...
And I interrogate myself, as many others like me
have also tried, as their best pages are cut
and ripped away. I would like ...

I would like to forget, because the dead
should not speak to the living,
should not push themselves into their lives.

THEORY OF ANDALUSIA

You say that I have lost my roots,
and that may well be so;
that in the images of my poetry,
mute and sombre,
there is no blue sky
nor white houses
nor black silhouette
of the old woman in her door
on the sad streets of our land.
You tell me
that I have not drawn the sense of Andalusia
into the pulse of my search,
into the beat of my heart.
Perhaps it is so. But do not think
that I do not feel the pain
when I run my hands over the wounded map
of our land,
like a blind man groping towards the light.
And do not think that I cannot tell
the intense perfume of the South
from the false scent
that others make her wear.
My brother, that is not the point; at night
Andalusia comes to me
not with the strident voice of the guitar
nor through a courtyard of tiles,
but through the darkness,
Andalusian as well,
of wounded pain and silent waiting,
and the tears

of your wife, her eyes fixed upon the ceiling,
your children now lost and alone,
just as I am lost for ever
when in the greyest dawn
their guns bring down another tree.
And if we talk of trees,
what other tree more pensive,
more fearful or more outraged
than the simple olive of the mountain grove,
twisted in grief and pain?
How then can I deny Andalusia?
That is not the point, comrade.
But circumstances led me to anchor in a different port,
and perhaps no port is possible in this storm
for the poet is the stepchild of exile;
and on my journey
only in the heart of this prison cell
have I found the warm air
and shared bread of that Andalusian sky,
luminous, profound, whose aroma,
Eduardo,
you tell me is mine: is ours.

THEORY OF LOVE

And if time and space are folds
on that dark robe of Destiny
that so many dress as God, and which cross
two lovers starred to love
before fortune begins its play,
then with what presumption the lover
who loves and who is loved
centres the cosmos upon himself,
becomes the lynchpin upon which countless angels dance.
My love was born in times to come,
and our short lives ran
their parallel course: geometry so rigid
we missed our entrances and exits,
our promised happy end. What if not vanity
spawned the passion of Romeo for his Juliet?
Was it only their cup, and theirs alone,

which brimmed with tears?
Perhaps in the wholeness of being
which we call woman, that they call man
– for all else is the anecdote of a single day –
the hidden truth may lie; each casual encounter
transforms into body and blood
in the eucharist of the senses
the communion of all mankind;
that the tender dialectic of sex
is whole, and held, Alicia,
in my repose in you,
in yours in me.

27th SEPTEMBER

Whilst I fought with my aching head's fragility,
in a punishment cell locked away,
they cut down wheat of life at break of day,
uprooted five young ears of corn. Nobility

and error now without redemption. There is no beauty.
There is no beauty in what I have to say.
Five stone bodies that bear witness today
I raise over this abyss of brutality.

Spain, my land, my home, why do you turn
your tragic gaze upon one whose task
is to reflect in his own eyes your grace?

Show us the naked purity of your dawn,
tear off the bloodied mask
that disfigures your untroubled face.

A TALE OF TWO CITIES

Dreams, love, our intentions
are places of passage. The hangover
that comes in the wake of memory, must it always

carry the taste of bitter almond?
I remember that quayside, that pure
transparent morning,
the clusters of working boats
from marine rivers,
and on the clear smooth skin of the air
the silver voice of the bell,
its peal lodged within ...
... the nostalgia of the moment.
Was everything really so white that day?
So much quicklime at home and in the heart?
Perhaps not; but unconcerned
that I would later mourn what was far behind
I left that solid place ... weighing the anchor
held by time's drifting sands;
like keys into a well, I tossed
moorings onto the broken back
of the sleeping sea,
not with the snap of a whip
but with the salt kisses of hope.

And landfall today in an unknown place,
cold dawn in this strange city. The dark
calm of its waters a world
from the risks of storm
brooding in the veins of my own sea.
Colours fading away:
the grey quayside, the grey disquiet
of the sharpening shadows of vessels of war ...
and in the words
that I hear and cannot understand
there is the deadness of the grey weight
of silence.
No less a place of passage? I have roamed
its ancient streets, twisted and soured
with wine, streets with gaze averted:
the sorrowing streets of a city whose silence
takes root and grows,
... and as I walk
through them, slowly turning from house
to house like one whose eyes waken from dream
to day; then with bitter memory
I know again: these are my people:
this my city, and this my land.

ANOTHER HISTORY LESSON

All of history has been a terrible misunderstanding.
Today if Crassus and Spartacus shared
a pint in the pub, Crassus freed from the purpledom of power
and the stench of blood, Spartacus from the fetters
hobbling him before the final blow,
they would chat in idle tranquillity,
wondering amused, amazed
at how and why, the influence of what minutiae
spurred their lives along such different paths.
(Lady Macbeth was wrong to believe the perfumes
of Arabia powerless to purify her hand,
cleanse it of the touch of death. Time is enough,
with perhaps the dark-scented shroud of an accomplice or two
to cover the tracks of crime.)
Auschwitz was a mistake; Chatilla and Sabra
nothing more than the graceless gesture
of an actor new to the boards,
but who will come to dominate the stage
and simply put his past behind him,
let is grow grey in the distance. Nobody
every knew burning inquisition for denying the teachings
of a Pope; and in any case
it makes no sense to hold hard
to a living image of what is little more
than mere anecdote, ageing now,
a simple misunderstanding
which has had no lasting effect
on our progress to the neutron bomb,
to the cold smile of passion contained, to the vital
approbation behind which we shelter,
and where nothing speaks of the horror
I recall here and at this split second;
for my children and yours will also forget one day
over a pint in the pub,
without memory.

Polygon

FICTION

In Between Talking about the Football
Gordon Legge

Music and football: the twin peaks of existence in these stories of urban life, by the author of *The Shoe*.
September   0 7486 6112 3
£7.95   144pp · Pb

darkness throws down the sun
peter plate

A dazzling novel from the U.S. Traces the birth of a revolutionary to his death in a prison uprising.
October   0 7486 6117 4
£7.95   136pp   Pb

The Man Who Came Back
Essays and Short Stories
Neil M. Gunn

A new collection with the emphasis on Scottish tradition and identity.
September   0 7486 6114 X
£8.95   172pp   Pb

POETRY

Scots Baronial
John Dixon

A debut collection, at times satirical, lyrical, optimistic and despairing.
November   0 7486 6124 7
£6.95   96pp   Pb

DETERMINATIONS

Strategies for Self-Government
James Mitchell

Exploring the strategies deployed by the Scottish National Movement in its attempt to establish a Scottish Parliament.
October   0 7486 6113 1
£8.95   160pp   Pb

The Manufacture of Scottish History
Ian Donnachie & Christopher Whately

A critical look at recent Scottish historiography.
January   0 7486 6120 4
£8.95   160pp   Pb

GENERAL

The Shadow and its Shadow
Surrealist Writing on Cinema
Edited by Paul Hammond

The Surrealists on their passion for moviegoing with contributions from Dalí, Buñuel, and Man Ray.
September   0 7486 6115 8
£9.95   160pp   Pb

Against Art and Artists
Jean Gimpel

A pungent attack on the art establishment and its apparent disregard for moral, social, and economic problems.
October   0 7486 6123 9
£8.95   160pp   Pb

The Sang's the Thing
The Disappearing Generation
Sheila Douglas

An oral history of the vanishing world of bothy boys and balladeers, accompanied with their songs. Illustrated.
November   0 7486 6119 0
£9.95   160pp   Pb

<u>Polygon</u>

Radical Renfrew
Edited by Tom Leonard
'remarkable and valuable anthology' *Scotsman*
'*Radical Renfrew* is the most significant event
in Scottish Poetry for a very long time.' *Glasgow Herald*
Paperback   0 7486 6028 3   £9.95

Collected Poems 1964-87
D.M. Black
Meditative poems culled from previous books and
poetry magazines, this collection ranges over themes of
religion and the tensions between the sexes.
Paperback   0 7486 6089 5   £9.95   March

Ophelia and other Poems
Elizabeth Burns
The first collection of poems from an Edinburgh poet, whose
tender tones sometimes are exchanged for an incensed
reminder of those who cannot make themselves heard.
Paperback   0 7486 6096 8   £6.95   March

22 George Square . Edinburgh EH8 9LF
Tel: 031 662 0553 . Fax: 031 662 0053

In the Face of Eternity
Edited by Christopher Whyte
A new generation of Gaelic poets at work. Includes poems from Aonghas MacNeacail, Meg Bateman and Maoilios Caimbeul.
Paperback   0 7486 6091 7   £9.95

Edinburgh University Press

European Poetry in Scotland
An Anthology of Translations
Edited by Peter France and Duncan Glen
'full of unexpected pleasures' *Books in Scotland*
'a fine book'   Iain Crichton Smith
'a collection of exceptional interest' *SLJ*
Now in paperback   0 85224 625 0   £9.50

An Anthology of Scottish Women Poets
Edited by Catherine Kerrigan
Over 70 poems from the Middle Ages to the present day, in Gaelic, Scots and English, put Scottish women's poetry firmly on the literary map.
Paperback   0 7486 0234 7   £12.95
Cased   0 7486 0125 2   £25.00   July

OUT FROM BENEATH THE BOOT
(issue 2)

an anthology of radical poetry

edited by Bobby Christie

published by Neruda Press

£ 2.95

ISBN 9516049 2 9

distributed by
A.K.DISTRIBUTION
3 BALMORAL PLACE
STIRLING
SCOTLAND

A third issue of

OUT FROM BENEATH THE BOOT

will be published shortly

by

Neruda Press
51 Allison Street
Glasgow G42 8NG
Scotland

contributions for future issues welcome.
please send a stamped, self-addressed envelope
with any work.

contributors to issue 2 are: John Duffy, Robert Fulton,
Ronald McNeil, James McSharry, Ronnie Smith, Rodney R Relax,
John Daley, Mary J. McCann, Michael Horovitz, William Oliphant,
Janet Finlayson, Mary McNally, William Gilfedder, Paul Birtill,
Debbie White, Brian Whittingham, Jim Ferguson, Alex Lambert,
John McGarrigle, Alison Reid, Jim Craig, Margaret Millmaker,
Brendan Cleary, Gini Craig, Margaret M. McCauslan,
Alistair MacKinnon, Bobby Christie, Bobby Sands.

Cybernetics

David Mackenzie

Part One: Learning to Walk

THE MAN LYING on his side at the bottom of the steps leading into the underground station is still moving his legs in long slow strides. The intermittent contact of the sides of his scuffed shoes with the grey concrete floor engages his body in a curious turning motion, his feet treading the circumference of a circle, his hips at the centre, his head and upper body moving backwards in awkward but relentless geometry.

The legs of the people rushing past him are involved in quick, accurate, effective movements, propelling bodies into the tunnel which opens out, farther on, into the station forecourt. Some of these people pause for a moment as they reach the man, glance down at him for a second or two to take in his young face and his brown, dusty coat. The stream of commuters parts, moves round on either side, joins again, moves on.

The place where the man is lying, the very point around which his body is slowly pivoting, is no more than fifteen feet from the road above the underpass. This road is also full of movement, manufactured and metallic, all four lanes braiding and rebraiding into a spillway of grimed metal and chrome. From the tunnel entrance the noise that is generated by these vehicles is rich and aggressive, an almost monotonous white roar into which individual mechanical sounds merge and submerge.

A tall slim man wearing a grey business suit and carrying an overfull briefcase comes down the steps, sees the young man lying on his side, passes him, walks quickly on for another ten or fifteen yards and then stops. He stands for a few moments, still facing his direction of travel. Then he turns and tries to make his way back to the tunnel entrance. This is difficult for him as he is going against the flow of people but he reaches the man eventually and leans down over him until their faces almost touch. The tall man's position further restricts movement into and out of the tunnel. He places his briefcase on the floor beside the young man whose cycling leg movements have almost ceased. Other briefcases brush the backs of the tall man's legs as he stands there, bent over, and tries to speak to the young man whose eyes, unfocussed, stare directly ahead of him. The noise from the roadway overhead and the bustle all round them makes communication between the two men very difficult. There appears to be no response at all from the young man. The tall man bends his knees and crouches down. He reaches out and takes hold of the young man's left shoulder. He begins to shake it, gently at first and then with gathering force as he notes no change in the condition of the young man's eyes, still staring ahead, fixed, if on anything, on an advertising poster which has been pasted to the tiny grey tiles of the tunnel wall.

A girl with short-cropped, pale blonde hair and wearing a white low-cut blouse is enjoying a bar of dark chocolate. Her bright red lips on which every tiny crease and fold of skin is visible, fit neatly round the end of the narrow chocolate bar from which the silver wrapping has been peeled back.

The tall man speaks again and this time there is a response in that the young man turns his head and tries to look at his new companion. The tall man takes hold of the young man's left arm and hauls him quickly to his feet. As he does this he notices a small white plastic bag on the floor, previously trapped under the young man's body. He leans the young man against the tunnel wall and steps back to the centre of the walkway to retrieve his own briefcase and this plastic bag in which there seem to be only a few light possessions. This manoeuvre requires him to step twice across the flow of people heading into the station and he receives two or three bumps and nudges.

Meanwhile the young man, only a matter of five or six feet away, begins to slip gently down the wall. His back remains vertical but his knees buckle very slowly so his descent is little more than a gradual and measured lessening of height until he is sitting on his heels. His eyes are still open, however, and he appears to be staring across at the blonde woman with the chocolate bar who can be glimpsed intermittently between the rushing bodies. The tall man sets the briefcase and the plastic bag down and, taking hold of the lapels of the young man's brown overcoat, pulls him to his feet again. The young man begins to tilt forward but a restraining hand pushes him gently back against the wall. With his upper arm thrust under the young man's left armpit trapping the left arm against his body, the tall man grasps the briefcase in his free hand and sets off into the tunnel. After two uncertain steps he halts, sets the briefcase down and presses the swaying figure of the young man back against the wall once more. He dashes back two or three yards to collect the plastic bag which he had failed to pick up. By the time he returns, the young man's knees have given way again and he has begun sliding towards the concrete floor. The tall man whisks him up, shifts the plastic bag to his other hand, grabs the briefcase in the same hand, whirls the young man round, pinions his arm in a strong grip and launches the two of them into the tunnel once again.

Their pace is dictated by the rate of the body flow around them and the uncertain movements of the young man who takes a few short steps followed by much longer ones. This disables any rhythm the tall man has managed to build up and changes them into a strange sideways tandem creature apparently struggling to find its feet.

They reach the bright station forecourt. The concrete floor gives way to speckled grey tiles, scuffed by thousands of feet. The sound of the traffic above has subsided but is replaced, below them, by the clatter of the silver-grey underground trains as they burst from the tunnels. There is more movement too as another pedestrian entryway can be seen from which even more people are disgorged into the forecourt. These people bring with them a hundred conversations which break, restart and break again as the several pathways cross and recross on the way to the ticket barrier. Automatic gates feed the passengers through to the crowded upper area from which the steps lead down on either side to the two platforms.

The tall man leans the young man against the small free area of wall near a kiosk where cigarettes and confectionery are on sale. The blonde woman is there, behind him, still consuming her chocolate. The young man's head, lolling backwards, strikes her on the nose. The tall man places the briefcase and plastic bag on the floor. He steps over to the kiosk and makes a purchase. By the time he retraces these few steps from the kiosk, the young man is sitting once again on his heels. The tall man leans over and holds out a chocolate bar in front of the young man's face. A few words come from the young man. The tall man straightens up, unwraps the chocolate bar completely and offers it to the young man. The sight of the chocolate bar galvanises him. He grabs it with his right hand and stuffs it into his mouth. Within a few seconds it has gone. A minimum of chewing has been employed. The tall man speaks again and the young man, still sitting on his heels and leaning against the wall with his knees at the level of his chin, nods. The tall man returns to the kiosk. The young man notices that there are crumbs of chocolate smeared on the fingers of his right hand. It is not clear whether he has caught sight of them – his eyes appear to be looking straight ahead, as before – or sensed their presence through his fingertips. He raises his hand to his face, thrusts all four fingers and thumb into his mouth and sucks them.

Then he sucks each finger separately, licking the tips in turn, ending with the thumb. By the time he has completed this exercise the tall man has returned from the kiosk bearing another bar of chocolate. This is consumed only slightly more slowly than the first.

The tall man waits patiently as the procedure of licking the fingers takes place as carefully and as methodically as before. Then he speaks again and the young man shakes his head. This interchange is repeated two or three times. The tall man squats down and talks in an earnest manner. At one point he opens the white plastic bag and looks through it. The young man's eyes close and his head slips to one side. The tall man reaches forward and grabs his collar. He gives it a shake but fails to get any response. He takes hold of each of the young man's ankles in turn and draws them forward so that he is now sitting on the grey speckled tiles with his legs stretched out before him.

The tall man rises and turns, apparently to go towards the ticket barrier. The kiosk owner notices this and shouts something at him. His few words are lost in the din as, below them, a train pulls into the station. There is a loud hiss as the doors are released and a hard rolling sound as they spring apart. The train is almost empty but a large crowd of commuters is waiting to board it.

At the door nearest the exit stairs a man in a grey tracksuit and holding a bicycle tries to get off the train against the crush of people trying to get on. One pedal of the bicycle snags a shopping basket which is pulled from the grasp of the middle-aged lady who is carrying it. The basket is dumped on the slatted wooden floor of the tube train. It contains mostly vegetables, including a plastic two-pound bag of new potatoes. This bag is ejected from the basket and splits as it hits the floor. The potatoes are all quite small and round and they scatter among the feet of those getting on the train.

One passenger, a businessman carrying a briefcase, steps on a potato which is squashed between the wooden slats of the floor but exudes enough juice to lubricate the sole of the highly polished shoe which pressurises it. The man slides sharply to the right, recovers momentarily and then pitches forward. He lets go of his briefcase and puts his hands out to break his fall. One corner of the briefcase strikes the floor first, the clips at the top spring apart with the shock and the briefcase flies open. The contents are deposited across the floor of the rapidly filling carriage.

A copy of the Financial Times, three pens, two pencils, a red and yellow packet containing thirty six photographs, a collapsible umbrella, a metal spectacle case, a dog-eared copy of *The Wilt Alternative,* a small plastic dispenser of Panadol tablets, a report on the Relative Processing Power of the IBM E, S and J series of multiprocessors, an out of date British Rail ticket to Milton Keynes, a keyring with five keys and a leather tab with 'Thailand' embossed on it, a small brown paper bag containing a wooden pepper mill and two tickets for the following evening's performance of 'Shirley Valentine' at the Empire Cinema, Leicester Square are all strewn over the floor along with at least half a dozen paper clips.

Three or four passengers bend down to help retrieve the contents of both the briefcase and the shopping basket while someone else helps the man who has fallen to get to his feet. He inspects his hands which are scuffed and bruised but not bleeding.

The cyclist, meanwhile, has managed to extricate himself from the crowd and is standing at the back of the platform waiting for the crush to subside. He has seen nothing of the incident with the shopping basket and the briefcase. He leans his bicycle against the wall and inspects it for signs of damage. The man in the train has now recovered his briefcase and all its contents except the paper clips. From his position in the centre of the space between the doors of the carriage he looks out over the heads of those latecomers still struggling to get on and sees the cyclist over by the wall, or rather, predominantly the cyclist's backside as he leans over to check the chain and gearing. Growing out of the cyclist's back is a large chocolate bar, partly unwrapped and angled towards the red lips of the blonde girl, her eyes apparently fixed on the man on the train.

The public address system barks a warning.

The lady with the shopping basket is still missing some items, notably most of the potatoes, at least one of which has been trampled on. She tries to look round for some of these but the carriage is now completely full of people and no further movement is possible.

There is a hiss as the doors prepare to close. One potato has lodged in the door runnel. The left hand door reaches it first and sends it tumbling along the groove until it meets the right hand door and is abruptly squashed quite flat.

From the platform the cyclist looks up the steps to the ticket barrier and station concourse above. When there appears to be a lull in the number of commuters descending the steps he picks up his bicycle and makes his way up. He takes it slowly and there is no further incident. When he reaches the top, however, he is faced with the problem of negotiating the automatic ticket gates as there is no ticket collector at either of the ticket barriers, both of which are firmly closed. He looks around and finally catches sight of the ticket collector who is standing by the kiosk in a group which includes three other figures. These are the tall man, the kiosk owner and the young man who is still sitting upright on the floor but with his head leaning over on his shoulder.

The tall man and the kiosk owner are both talking at the same time and both are gesticulating though the gestures of the kiosk owner are more abrupt and agitated. The ticket collector has his hands in his pockets. He is standing with his feet apart and he occasionally goes over on his ankles so that his full weight is taken on the outer edges of sole and heel.

The young man slips to one side and as he steadies himself with his hand he knocks over the tall man's briefcase. A young boy, perhaps twelve or thirteen years old, trips over the briefcase and sprawls on the floor. As he falls he makes a grab for the nearest object which is a display bin of chocolate bars positioned to one side of the kiosk. His hand rakes the top of the display and several chocolate bars are flung to the floor. The kiosk owner turns to yell at the boy. The boy picks up himself and three chocolate bars and sprints for one of the exits. One of the other dislodged bars has struck the young man on the knee and landed on the tiled floor at his side. He gives a long, slow shrug and reaches for the bar. The kiosk owner, intent on picking up the other bars scattered on the floor, does not notice the one which the young man is now struggling to unwrap.

The kiosk owner rejoins the tall man and the ticket collector and continues to argue. His voice rises to a shout but is lost in the clamour as another train pulls into the station. The young man continues to work at the wrappings of the chocolate bar but its pressed and glued seams are too much for his awkward and uncoordinated fingers. The bar falls to the floor between his legs two or three times and he appears to pick it up with less enthusiasm on each occasion.

Finally, with a dismissive gesture, the kiosk owner turns abruptly from the tall man and re-enters his kiosk. The tall man now fixes his attention on the ticket collector but he has already turned away as the cyclist has finally managed to catch his eye. The tall man is left alone with the young man. He crouches down in front of him again but as he does so the young man's upper body slowly keels over and he slumps onto the floor beside the kiosk.

The still unwrapped chocolate bar falls from his lap onto the floor. The kiosk owner, a witness to the young man's collapse, comes from his kiosk and stands over the two figures, the tall man crouched down and the young man recumbent. The tall man looks up and he and the kiosk owner exchange a look but no words. Then the kiosk owner leans over and retrieves the chocolate bar from beside the young man's knees. He returns to the kiosk, replacing the bar on the display bin as he does so.

The ticket collector opens the barrier to allow the cyclist and his bicycle through onto the station forecourt. He checks the cyclist's ticket and returns it to him. Seeing the barrier open, a number of passengers who have just got off the most recent train move away from the automatic ticket gates and attempt to follow the cyclist. The ticket collector tries to close the barrier against them but he is too late. As the train clanks and wheezes its way out of the station below them he shouts at the passengers and points over to the automatic gates. He is ignored. So many people rush past him that he has difficulty checking more than a few tickets. The tall man approaches the ticket collector from behind and speaks into his ear. Without turning round the ticket collector waves him away. The tall man moves round until he is at the ticket collector's shoulder, partly blocking the exit through which passengers continue to push and shove their way. He speaks earnestly perhaps heatedly to the ticket collector who has given up any attempt to close the barrier and is concentrating hard on grabbing as many tickets as possible. The tall man persists, gesticulating towards the young man lying motionless beside the kiosk. His manner is becoming almost violent and he is beginning to shout.

A woman of about twenty, wearing a black sweater and faded blue jeans and with her brown hair braided into a long pigtail, rushes through the barrier, passing as far away from the ticket collector as the narrow exit will allow. The ticket collector spots her, turns, pushes the tall man roughly out of the way and yells at her to stop. She continues to move away, however, walking as fast as she can without actually breaking into a run. She heads for one of the station exits, sees the young man on the floor by the kiosk and stops abruptly.

She goes over to him, crouches down in front of him and sniffs the air before his face. She looks round and catches the eye of the tall man who is standing behind the ticket collector again as more people veer away from the automatic gates and make for the ticket barrier. The tall man walks quickly over to her and leans towards her, hands on knees, to talk to her. Together they pull the young man into an upright position and the tall man tries to prop him up by taking his heavy briefcase and setting it on end underneath the young man's right arm.

A few moments later they are joined by the ticket collector who has seen the rush of passengers through and has managed to close the ticket barrier. He grabs the girl by the arm and yanks her to her feet. She gives a little scream of surprise and wrenches her arm free.

The ticket collector starts shouting. The tall man steps between them, facing the ticket collector. He holds his hands up, palms outward, and seems about to place them on the ticket collector's shoulders.

The next train clatters into the station. The ticket collector continues to shout, though a little less loudly, and keeps pointing past the tall man at the girl behind. There are moments when he seems about to reach round and grab the girl but the tall man keeps his body between the two and carries on talking in a soft voice which at times is lost in the background noise of the newly arrived train, the ticket gates, the announcements and the movement of hundreds of people. His right hand touches lightly the ticket collector's left shoulder. The ticket collector stops talking and appears to be listening. The tall man puts his head to one side and talks calmly.

The first passengers from the most recent train arrive at the automatic gates.

The young girl cowers behind the tall man.

The young man slips sideways to his left.

The ticket collector folds his arms across his chest.

Someone shouts from the ticket barrier.

Amid the din, the ticket collector says something quite quietly.

The tall man takes some coins from his pocket and hands them over to the ticket collector.

The train grinds its way out of the station.

There are more shouts from the ticket barrier.

The girl pokes her head round from behind the tall man. She points over to the young man who is slumped on the floor again.

The kiosk owner shouts something as another train bursts from the tunnel.

The ticket collector turns and walks slowly towards the ticket barrier. He opens it, steps back and lets the crowd of people rush through. He makes no attempt to check any tickets. He leaves the gate wide open and walks slowly to a small wooden cubicle at the far side of the forecourt. Inside the cubicle there is a stool and a ledge. On the ledge there is a telephone. The ticket collector taps the wall above the phone twice with his knuckle. Then he picks up the receiver and begins to dial.

COMMON SENSE

Journal Of Edinburgh Conference Of Socialist Economists

10

THIS ISSUE:

Philip Agee, formerly of the CIA, on why the U.S. needed the Gulf War • The Student Debt Crisis • Elisabeth Behrens on workers' struggles under National Socialism • A tribute to Scottish miners • Poetry by Bryan Duncan and Jim Ferguson • Harry Cleaver on Argentinian Gouchos • The Trafalgar Square Defendants' Campaign's report on the policing of anti-poll tax demonstrations

Issue 10 • £3.95   Subscription to Issues 10, 11 and 12 • £12.00 (£6.00 unwaged rate).   Please send cheque/postal order payable to 'Common Sense'. Overseas: please send Bankers Draft or International Money Order for   £15.00 sterling (£10.00 unwaged rate).

Order/Subscription Address
Common Sense
PO Box 311   S.D.O
Edinburgh EH9 1SF
Scotland

IDEAS

CHARLES STEPHENS
MALCOLM GREEN
LORNA J. WAITE
ANNE W. MULLEN
JAMES RUSSELL GRANT

£1512: The Ceramic Workshop Edinburgh

Charles Stephens

Three Statements

I

The sum of £1512 represents the remaining funds of Ceramic Workshop Edinburgh whose operations were frustrated in 1974 by unforeseeable and insuperable financial obstacles.

The Executive Committee of Ceramic Workshop Edinburgh have therefore resolved –

that all remaining funds of the Workshop shall become the medium of an art work;

that those funds shall be invested by the Committee to earn interest;

that the interest earned shall be added to those funds;

that those funds and the added earned interest shall not be drawn from in the future;

that the annual audit of this activity shall be published annually as a signed, limited edition;

that the Committee shall be the protectors and the promoters of the art work.

The remaining funds are £1512 and have been invested: the investment certificates are locked into a black attache case.

The complete art work – *£1512* – comprises the activity generated by the entombed sum of money.

The Committee of Ceramic Workshop Edinburgh
4th February 1977

II

The Ceramic Workshop is a non-profit-distributing art organisation. Founded in 1970 it provided facilities and technical advice for artists, potters and students. To subsidise this cultural and educational venture the Workshop marketed a wide range of ceramic materials and studio equipment.

The Ceramic Workshop, as an open-studio and materials supplier, closed in 1974, and, after all creditors and grants were repaid, there remained a residual sum of £1,512. In 1977 this sum was invested by the Workshop Committee in Treasury Bonds, with the proviso that neither the capital nor the interest would ever be drawn upon. The documents and the certificates relating to the investment were lodged in a black attache case.

The audited accounts, which are published as a limited edition print, show for 1987-88 that the net assets are £5,806 and keeping abreast of the 1977 computer forecast that the net assets of The Workshop would be doubled every five years, and would surpass £400,000,000 by the year 2077.

Created by the artist and advisers of The Workshop, £1512 was first exhibited in the Roxburghe Hotel, Edinburgh in 1977. It was then lodged with the Scottish National Gallery of Modern Art and has since been loaned to a number of international exhibitions; most notably the Museum des Geldes in the Kunsthalle, Dusseldorf, which then toured to Centre Pompidou, Paris and other European centres.

The Committee of Ceramic Workshop Edinburgh
23rd September 1988

III

I have chosen it [£1512] because it is about yesterday, today and tomorrow – and because it has a very slow fuse.'

George Wyllie explaining why £1512 *was the President's Choice for the SSA Annual Exhibition at the Royal Scottish Academy Sept-Oct 1988*

Ten Propositions

1. '£1512' is a work of art.
2. It was created by a committee.
3. It consists of an idea which is expressed through the medium of money.
4. Its material representation takes the form of a black attache case which contains investment certificates and a series of annual bank statements of account which are issued as a limited edition print.
5. It is abstract.
6. It is also concrete – nothing is more substantial than money.
7. It is a drawing – the line of a graph which maps the progress of an investment through time.
8. It is a sculpture – the moulding of part of the substance of the world into a form.

9. It is not as familiar to the public as it could be.

10. It is the product of the mutual interaction of two processes which are analogous to those of differential and integral calculus.

The structure of '£1512' can therefore be expressed, in quasi-mathematical terms, as follows:

$g'(\text{art}) = g(\text{money})$ where $g(\text{money})$ is a quantity of money and $g(\text{art})$ is an art work. $g'(\text{art})$ is the derived function of $g(\text{art})$ at a given time t. This derived function at time t may be expressed as a quantity of money. This equation could be translated into ordinary language by the phrase:

ART IS MONEY

$\int g(\text{art}) = g(\text{idea})$ where $g(\text{idea})$ is a concept and $g(\text{art})$ is an art work. $\int g(\text{art})$ is the integral of the function $g(\text{art})$ over the whole period and extent of its operation. This integral may be expressed as a concept. This equation could be translated into ordinary language by the phrase:

ART AS IDEA

Art is money

The Ceramic Workshop was, and still is, an attempt to transform the profits of a business into art.

The seeds which eventually grew into the Ceramic Workshop were probably sown during a number of conversations which took place during 1968 and 1969 between Merilyn Smith, who was teaching Ceramics at the Edinburgh College of Art, and Professor Jim McKinnel, a visiting lecturer from the USA. McKinnel made a significant contribution to the genesis of the Ceramic Workshop. Together with five others, he had recently published a series of articles which revealed the technological and craft 'secrets' of ceramics in the USA. This act, which had been co-ordinated to take place in a single week, broke the 'closed shop' of the ingrown world of ceramics. It confirmed Smith in her conviction that techniques and expertise could be as important, as assets, as the design and making of a finished product. McKinnel also told her of workshops in the USA which had been set up and run as successful small businesses by ceramists. When she told him of her ideas for setting up a workshop in Edinburgh, McKinnel's enthusiasm and practical support were invaluable. Along with Eduardo Paolozzi and Michael Cardew, McKinnel was to become an honorary member of the committee of the Ceramic Workshop.

Smith had clear and ethical principles about art. These formed the basis of everything which the Ceramic Workshop was to achieve. The daughter of an Arbroath pharmacist, she believed that art should share the values of science. It ought to be concerned with research and knowledge. Its findings should be precisely expressed and freely exchanged. It should be about possibilities rather than dogmas, about processes rather than results. Art objects should be by-products of these things, and not end-products. There need not be any visible product at all. Smith believed that, like science research programmes whose ends were dictated by government or industry, art which was obsessed with generating objects would quickly lose its creativity. In order to avoid this deadening pressure, it was necessary for art to be financially independent. Smith, inspired by McKinnel's example, believed that she could use her technical expertise in ceramics to generate a profit, from preparing and selling raw materials and from acting as a technical consultant, which could be used to support a workshop dedicated to her rigorous artistic philosophy. With the support of McKinnel and the active assistance of her husband Alan, a painter, she set out to turn her ideas into reality.

Smith's first idea was to set up a centre which would involve all of the arts. Expertise, equipment, materials and knowledge could be concentrated under one roof. She envisaged this project as a blending together of a workshop, a studio and a university of the arts. She had a particular building in mind – an old school at the top of the Royal Mile.

It was not to be. Smith and her partner, her husband Alan, had energy and enthusiasm, but they had no financial resources of their own. Their sponsor was not initially prepared to think on anything other than a modest scale. That sponsor was the Scottish Arts Council.

The Scottish Arts Council had been set up in 1968 by Jenny Lee, the Minister for the Arts of the second Wilson government. Like the Kilbrandon Commission (1968-73), the SAC was an important element in the package of measures which made up the Wilson Government's response to the upsurge of Scottish Nationalism in the mid 1960s. The SAC was not set up in a vacuum. The 1960s had been an outstanding time for the visual arts in Scotland. In 1960, the National Gallery of Modern Art was established. In 1963 the Traverse Gallery opened and in 1966 the Richard Demarco Gallery set out on its extraordinary career. In 1967, Ian Hamilton Finlay started his Wild Hawthorn Press and in 1969 he moved to Little Sparta to begin work on his 'neo-classical' garden.

In late 1969, when Smith was looking for funds for her project, the SAC was up and running. Other sources of finance were few and far between. Industry and commerce had comparatively little interest in the arts in those days, and it was most unlikely that they would have entertained the idea of backing the risky early stages of a project like the Ceramic Workshop. Smith would have had no difficulty in getting commercial backing for an enterprise which produced finished ceramics, but her objective was to create a workshop whose final product was open and undetermined. Technical skills, ceramic expertise and a thriving material supplies business rather than an output of finished pots, ornaments and tiles were to create a financial base which would in turn provide creative freedom for artists. The Scottish Development Department and the Highlands and Islands Development Board might have provided funds for a project of that kind on Loch Morar, but they had no remit in over-developed Edinburgh. Smith turned to the SAC. They were interested, but only in a modest project and only in a very cautious investment. Smith needed a £5000 loan for a five year period in order to set the business on its feet. The SAC offered her £1000 to support the workshop aspect of the project. They specified that the money should not go towards the business. This was absurd, since Smith had always conceived the two as being mutually interdependent.

The SAC's support was inadequate, but there was no alternative. As a result of its failure to secure a proper capital loan, the Ceramic Workshop, like the majority of arts organisations in Scotland, became an annual suitor for the favours of the SAC. A one-off start-up loan, such as might be provided by an Enterprise Allowance today, would have been the most appropriate response to the Ceramic Workshop's initial application. The SAC, like all bureaucracies, seemed to prefer dependent 'clients' to fledgling enterprises. It was, apparently, determined to keep the tightest of holds on the purse strings.

In one respect, the Ceramic Workshop had been extremely fortunate. It had obtained premises for a very modest rent. They were situated close to the centre of the Edinburgh Old Town, at 15-16 Victoria Terrace, perched just above the Grassmarket and just below Edinburgh Castle. Thanks to the generosity of a patron, Elaine Caplan, who loaned it £1000 for the purpose, the Ceramic Workshop was able to acquire the freehold of this very desirable property. The loan was paid back within a few months.

Smith had researched, with great thoroughness, all of the possible sources of clay and other raw materials in Scotland and the potential customers for such material. She tested each sample of clay, which she received from scores of locations all over the country, and by blending them she devised a selection which would satisfy the needs of her potential customers – schools, colleges and private users. Scottish ceramists almost invariably obtained their clay from Stoke-on-Trent.

The long transportation distance, combined with the fact that plastic clay was approximately 25% water, added a significant cost to the material. The clay supplied by the Ceramic Workshop, originating from somewhat closer to home, would avoid this handicap. This economic logic underpinned the viability of the Ceramic Workshop as a business. By the time that the Ceramic Workshop opened its doors for trading, Smith and her husband had prepared a catalogue of the goods and services which the Workshop would offer. Everything was ready to go.

The soundness of Smith's research into the opportunities available in Scotland for a supplier of clay, glazes and professional advice about kilns and other problems of ceramic working was quickly confirmed. Within two years, the Ceramic Workshop had established itself as a successful small business. The problems which faced it after the initial stresses of the start-up were typical of those faced by many small businesses. The Ceramic Workshop soon found it difficult, even impossible, to cope with the amount of business which came its way. It was often obliged to turn away customers.

It was consistent with the whole philosophy of the Ceramic Workshop that its base should have been 'horizontal' rather than vertical. The idea was that artists, and those who wanted, on a *personal* basis, to have a close involvement with the 'making' and 'support' of art, should be in charge. It was intended that the Ceramic Workshop should not be subjected to the restrictions which were inherent in the vertical patronage of governments, arts councils, business corporations, educational trusts or any other institutions. The Ceramic Workshop was an attempt to take art out of its marginalised ghetto and place it within society. The idea was that the Ceramic Workshop would act as a centre in which basic research into the technology, philosophy and language of art could be pursued. It would be a place in which artists could function in the manner of any small business or profession, but still work in accord with the highest precepts of the idea which is called 'art'. One of the principal intentions of the Ceramic Workshop was to demonstrate that artists had the kinds of expertise and insight which would be as relevant and appropriate to public service as those of any other profession. Planning committees and other public bodies included, as a matter of course, councillors, architects, public health officials and other accredited 'experts', but artists were never included in their professional capacity. It was intended that the success of the Ceramic Workshop should play an important part in changing this situation. This ambition was well reflected in the composition of the committee of the Ceramic Workshop.

The Ceramic Workshop had begun as an idea in the head of one person, Merilyn Smith, but it would have come to nothing at all without the commitment and unstinting belief of its committee. Although it was financially vulnerable, the Ceramic Workshop possessed a great fund of goodwill and practical resources in its committee and in the invaluable contribution of Moira McAndrew who ran the office and the gallery.

The following were members of the committee:
Bob Callender (Painter/Lecturer)
Graeme Murray (Sculptor)
Cordelia Oliver (Painter/Writer)
Iain Robertson (Teacher) Secretary
Andrew McLeod (Industrial Designer)
Anne Harris (Economist/University Lecturer) Treasurer
Archie Smith (Company Secretary) Chair
Alan Smith (Painter)

Between 1970 and 1974, Merilyn Smith was the manager of the Ceramic Workshop and therefore an employee, not a member, of the committee.

But in 1974 came financial crisis. Until then the support of its committee had enabled the Ceramic Workshop to achieve most of its objectives. When the crisis came, the committee bore the full brunt of its force but its unity was unshaken. Out of the original members of the committee, four (Merilyn Smith, Anne Miller (formerly Harris), Iain Robertson and Cordelia Oliver) remain members. The present composition of the committee of the Ceramic Workshop is as follows: Merilyn Smith (Artist/Lecturer Liverpool College of Art)(Chair); Iain Robertson (Senior Officer Scottish Council for Consultancy on the Curriculum)(Secretary); Anne Miller (Economist/Lecturer Heriot-Watt University)(Treasurer); Cordelia Oliver (Artist/Writer); Murdoch Lothian (Art Historian/Gallery Owner); Hilary Robertson (Sociologist/Lecturer).

The committee of the Ceramic Workshop, which now protects and promotes £1512, continues to meet regularly. The Ceramic Workshop is a living demonstration of the fact that loyalty and unity of purpose are more lasting than institutional patronage of the kind dispensed by the SAC and similar organisations.

What happened was this: the chronic weakness of the financial position of the Ceramic Workshop meant that it was unable to expand in accord with its growing reputation. It also meant that it was vulnerable to any adverse developments in its own, or indeed the general, financial situation. In order to pay for its stock, the Ceramic Workshop had been obliged to run a current account deficit. It had no capital resources of its own and was therefore obliged to negotiate substantial overdraft facilities with its bank. This went well enough between 1970 and 1973. Those were the years of the so-called Barber Boom when bank credit policy was more relaxed than at any time since 1945. This meant that overdrafts could be obtained, by small businesses such as the Ceramic Workshop, on what were, historically, very easy terms. It was believed, erroneously, that cheap credit was the best way to stimulate economic growth. In late 1973, not only did the Barber policies collapse with the inevitable consequence of a sharp tightening of credit control, but the great world economic Boom which had underwritten affluence, *and the arts*, since the early 1950s, came to a very messy end.

The crisis which led to the closing of the Ceramic Workshop unfolded against, and was influenced by, these portentous economic events. The bank manager who had been handling the Ceramic Workshop's affairs died. No doubt influenced by the inflationary presuppositions of the Barber years, he had been prepared to permit the Ceramic Workshop to persist in its current account overdraft. His successor, chastened by the gruesome economic events of the winter of 1973-4, was not prepared to extend the Ceramic Workshop's overdraft facilities. He was distinctly unimpressed by the idea of a small business which invested its profits in art. On June 15 1974 he gave the committee just eleven days to clear the Ceramic Workshop's overdraft of £4,000. The Ceramic Workshop was confronted, with virtually no warning, with foreclosure. It was not that it was a 'lame duck', to use the terminology of the time. In the four years since its inception in 1970, it had established itself as a viable business. Such achievements were unusual in the world of the arts. However, the events of the spring of 1974 were unprecedented. A government had fallen and the world economy was crashing into massive recession. There were more bankruptcies in 1974 than there had been at any time since 1931. Unlike Lonrho, the Ceramic Workshop was not primarily a business. Its bank manager had noted as much – to his displeasure. In these exceptional circumstances, the committee of the Ceramic Workshop sought help from a body whose whole raison d'etre was the support of the arts. They turned to the original sponsor of the Ceramic Workshop – the Scottish Arts Council.

The SAC had probably been affected by the atmosphere of economic crisis which surrounded the collapse of the Heath government, but it is worth remembering that there were no significant public service expenditure cuts until the Healey mini-Budget of July 1976. What is more, the advent of Scottish Oil, the presence of 7 SNP MPs at Westminster (a total which was increased to 11 after the October 1974 election) and the return to power of a Labour government very similar to that which had appeased Scottish opinion with the Kilbrandon Commission and other concessions (which had included the setting up of the SAC itself) in the much less intimidating Nationalist revival of 1966-68, could only strengthen the hand of the SAC when in the annual battle for funds. From March 1974, the Scottish National Party held the minority Labour government in the palm of its hand.

This unprecedented political situation offered great opportunities to Scottish lobbying groups such as the SAC. Indeed, in 1974, when the Ceramic Workshop was applying for assistance to rectify the crisis which had been precipitated by the changes in national Banking policy, the SAC was showing no signs of the effects of financial constraint or nervousness. On the contrary, whilst the United Kingdom was in the throes of its worst economic crisis since 1931, the SAC was involved in two ambitious projects – the setting up of the Third Eye Centre in Glasgow and the refurbishment of what was to become the Fruitmarket Gallery in Edinburgh. The eventual budget for these projects ran well into six figures, but both were completed without serious cuts.

It was somewhat ironical that, at the very moment when the SAC was taking ambitious initiatives on its own account, it should also have begun the long, and very messy, process of withdrawing its financial support from the Richard Demarco Gallery. The Richard Demarco Gallery had been set up in 1966 with the backing of private individuals. From 1968, it had begun to receive Scottish Arts Council support. This support had become steadily more significant between 1969 and 1973. Richard Demarco and the committee of the Richard Demarco Gallery, like the committee of the Ceramic Workshop, were autonomous individuals working to promote and protect the visual arts in Scotland. However, just like the Ceramic Workshop, he was grossly undercapitalised. This financial weakness created acute, and very dangerous, short term financial crises which in turn led to drastic cuts in programme budgets which invariably had disastrous implications for the complex international projects which *only* Demarco was capable of setting up. Like the Ceramic Workshop, Demarco needed a significant capital grant or else a guaranteed long-term commitment to funding by the SAC. Neither was forthcoming. As a result, he was obliged to close down his excellent Melville Square premises in March 1974 and move into a cramped basement in Great King Street. The SAC continued to fund Demarco, on a hand-to-mouth basis, for the rest of the 70s. In 1980, for very opaque reasons, they stopped his funding altogether and they have not restored it to anything like an adequate level in subsequent years. This ignominious murder by a thousand cuts might have been the fate of the Ceramic Workshop had it not decided, ruthlessly, to close its door in 1974 and so avoid a lingering death.

In 1974, the SAC, a bureaucracy, let down an individual, Demarco, whose contribution to contemporary art was recognised internationally. It also failed to protect a body, the Ceramic Workshop, whose originality and whose success its own officials had been only too happy to acknowledge when the going was easy. It has been pointed out that the crisis which engulfed the Ceramic Workshop in the Spring of 1974 and obliged its committee to ask the SAC for an emergency loan of £4000 had nothing to do with profligacy or incompetence. Now, one would have thought, was the time for the SAC to rally to the support of Scottish Art – in the form of the stricken Ceramic Workshop.

The negotiations and manoeuvres which followed are veiled in obscurity. The crucial SAC committee meetings which decided the fate of the Ceramic Workshop took place behind closed doors. It seems that there was never a general intention of the SAC to give the Ceramic Workshop the loan which it had requested. If this was so then it would have been consistent with the approach which the SAC had adopted when it refused to give the Ceramic Workshop more than a one year grant at the latter's inception in 1970. The final SAC offer of £2000 had all the appearance of an effort to throw money at an irritating problem rather than to address the realities of a very delicate situation. The SAC's preoccupation with the formidable demands of the Third Eye Centre and the Fruitmarket Gallery, together with the attitude which it had adopted towards Demarco at this time, suggest that it was most unlikely that it would have been prepared to get another 'independent' client off the hook.

The SAC's determination to control its clients seemed to be confirmed when Smith received an, apparently generous, offer to move the Ceramic Workshop, lock, stock and barrel, into the upstairs space at the refurbished Fruitmarket. As far as Smith and her colleagues were concerned, this was only adding insult to injury. The Ceramic Workshop owned a freehold on its own premises in Victoria Terrace, a much finer venue than the vicinity of Waverley Station and the *Scotsman* and *Evening News* printing works, which was the billet of the new Fruitmarket Gallery. The Ceramic Workshop had established a flourishing business network and it was well on the way to achieving its goal of becoming an independent centre, securely based in Scotland, where artists could manage and determine their own destiny independent of state, arts council and all other forms of sponsorship. The offer of a few rooms in the Fruitmarket Gallery either showed that the SAC did not have the first notion as to what the Ceramic Workshop was all about, or else that they had all too clear an idea. The SAC chose to see the Ceramic Workshop as a pleading, dependent, and probably whingeing, 'client', rather than as an autonomous body, dedicated to the arts in Scotland, which was the victim of an unforeseen national, indeed global, economic crisis. There is no doubt that a loan of £4000 would have saved the Ceramic Workshop, and all of the ideals which it represented. It would also have been repaid within a few years, as the economy as a whole slowly recovered from the crash of 1974 and the financial strains of rapid expansion, which had led to the Ceramic Workshop's liquidity crisis in the spring of that year, moderated.

If both the Ceramic Workshop and the Richard Demarco Gallery had been able to secure, and then afterwards sustain, their independence during this critical period, they could have formed the nucleus of an autonomous network for the distribution of visual arts funding in Scotland. In due course, this web of organisations which would have been run, by artists and in the interests of artists, could have provided an alternative to the SAC and to private business sponsorship. Today, there is no choice, or so it often seems, between the state and the private business sector as a source of support for the visual arts. It is interesting, and depressing, to realise that two of the most viable alternatives to this dismal state of affairs were, in the case of the Ceramic Workshop, destroyed and in the case of the Richard Demarco Gallery, wounded, in 1974, the very moment at which, in the eyes of many of its citizens, Scotland had attained a new self-confidence as a nation.

The SAC's offer of £2000 was inadequate. The committee of the Ceramic Workshop knew that it would not be improved upon and it was determined to avoid being subjected to the misery of hand-to-mouth funding which would be punctuated by arbitrary cuts and eventual termination. It also knew, that the SAC had, for one reason or another, failed to grasp the fact that the Ceramic Workshop was not some little gallery or craft shop whose overheads were modest and which might survive by judicious belt-tightening, or even a temporary closure. The Ceramic Workshop was a business and without a further £2000, it was a business which would go into liquidation. The committee had to prevent the creditors and debtors of the Ceramic Workshop from discovering the nature of the financial situation which had arisen as a consequence of the failure of the SAC to provide appropriate support. A period of silence was necessary so that the committee could square off the Ceramic Workshop's debts and call in its credits. If there was a public panic, then the creditors would call in their money and the debtors would not bother paying up. So it is with any business.

In the two years which followed the fiasco of the committee's application to the SAC, Merilyn Smith, as manager of the Ceramic Workshop, wound up the business side of the Ceramic Workshop with meticulous care. The Ceramic Workshop had ceased trading and therefore Smith, its manager, became redundant. She could not afford to pay the mortgage on the flat in which she, her husband, and her two young children lived, so it had to be sold. In 1967, she had fled with her family, in fear for all their lives, from the Civil War in Nigeria. They had arrived at Heathrow, carrying one large laundry basket and wearing everything else that they owned. They were refugees. The Ceramic Workshop had, to no small degree, sprung out of the desperation of that experience. It was an attempt to do something in the teeth of the chaos and antagonism of the world. In the months which followed the winding-up of the Ceramic Workshop, Smith felt that she and her family had become refugees once again. They left Edinburgh and moved to a remote part of Umbria.

When the winding up of the Ceramic Workshop's financial affairs was completed, a balance remained of £1,512. As they contemplated the ruin of over five years work and commitment, the members of the committee wondered how best to invest the sum for the benefit of art. Such a modest amount of capital could do little, if anything, to enable the Ceramic Workshop to resume its previous operations. It seemed absurd to buy a work of art with it and yet it could hardly be written off as petty cash, or buried away in some other accounting category, in order to create a final zero balance in the Ceramic Workshop accounts. This £1,512 was no ordinary sum of money. It was all that remained of the Ceramic Workshop and everything which it represented. It was all that remained of an attempt to liberate art from the bondage of money. The committee felt a violent resentment at the apparent failure of their enterprise. Despite all of their efforts, money had remained in control. The Ceramic Workshop had been overwhelmed by the collapse of the economy, by the attitude of its bank manager, by the feebleness of the financial support offered by the Scottish Arts Council. Money was the root and source of all of its ills. All that remained was money – £1,512.

The Ceramic Workshop came into existence so that the profits of a small business could be dedicated to art. The success of the Ceramic Workshop would have created a secure space in which art was protected from the distortions of corporate patronage, bureaucracy and the gallery system. The failure of this project meant that it was incumbent on the committee to protect the idea which had animated the Ceramic Workshop and to warn those that might attempt to follow its example of the dangers that lay in wait for them. The only means available to achieve this purpose was the balance of £1,512 and the power of art. £1,512 represented all that remained of the profit which would have been dedicated to art. It was logical that that sum of money should be the raw material out of which an admonitory work of art should be created.

Clay is transformed by being moulded into a form and then fired. Money is transformed by being invested. Just as firing turns raw clay into glazed ceramic, so investment, or rather the interest earned over a given period, turns money into a greater or smaller sum of money. The interest on a sum of money is therefore generated in a manner analogous to the process involved in the making of any work of art.

In this way, the £1,512 balance of the winding-up of the Ceramic Workshop became *£1512*, the art work. As the Ceramic Workshop was wound up, it was transformed. From its inception in 1970, it had, by the nature of its presuppositions, been concerned with the relationship between art and money. The Ceramic Workshop is perhaps best understood as a continuing art work, or art process, which is premised upon the unresolved dispute between art and money. In 1970, it took the form of a business whose profits were dedicated to art. On February 4 1977, it took the form of *£1512*, a sum of money whose accumulated earned interest *was* art.

Art as Idea

£1512 is a characteristic art work of the late twentieth century. Its form owes a great deal to a very particular development in twentieth century visual art which is often called conceptual art. Unlike impressionism, expressionism, cubism, abstraction and surrealism, conceptual art has been persistently, and often wilfully, misunderstood. The full resonance and subtlety of *£1512* cannot be appreciated without an understanding of this form of art.

Yves Klein (1928-62), Robert Smithson (1938-73) and Joseph Beuys (1921-86) are united by the fact that they are all 'conceptual' artists.

Between 1958 and 1962, Yves Klein 'made' a series of works which, superficially, might appear to have owed a great deal to the pranks of Dada and the Surrealists. They did not. Klein had nothing in common with that kind of thing. He was a man whose whole life was dedicated to philosophical research. A young man in a hurry, Klein concerned himself with many varieties of thought, ranging from those of Japan, India and the Orient to the philosophical Hermeticism and Gnosticism of the Alexandrine and Renaissance periods.

In 1958, Klein made *Le Vide* which consisted of an invitation to an exhibition which was a suite of empty rooms. *Le Vide* was no reworking of the fun and games of 'Relâche'. Klein was not a humorist. He was in earnest. He was pointing out, with exquisite precision, that art is not the artefact. Art, Klein was insisting, and not the vehicle which transmits it, is the work of art. The rest is secondary. This reasoning, and the precision of its form, an empty room, was worthy of the Wittgenstein of the *Philosophical Investigations*.

In 1960, in the series of *Anthropometries*, Klein developed his arguments in another direction. Implicit in *Le Vide* was the notion that the presence of the artist, rather than the art-object, was the defining principle. Traditional art 'represented' the human figure, landscape or architecture in a 'depictive' manner. 'Abstract' painting had refined the procedure. Klein extended the logic of abstraction until it reached the terminus of *Le Vide* in which only the artist, abstracted into 'will', was 'represented'. *Anthropometries* turned this 'abstraction' on its head, but with true dialectical skill Klein elegantly avoided a return to the past. Always insisting on the primacy of the human presence, Klein decided to make 'representional' art works which would, quite literally, be generated by the physical presence, the body, of the model. With a nod and a wink to Manet, Degas and Gauguin, Klein, the 'conceptualist' made a series of 'classical' nudes. He covered his female models with blue paint (blue for Klein was the colour of infinity and heaven) and let them down onto the emptiness of a white canvas. Their bodies created the image. Klein had made a painting of a nude, which, in as intimate and erotic a manner as a portrait by Renoir or Bonnard, recorded a human presence in the universe. At a stroke, Klein revealed that abstraction had not reached a formalistic dead end. Like an experiment in Physics, Klein's *Anthropometries* demonstrated that the future of 'art' was as open and as undetermined as it had ever been.

In the *Cosmogenies* (1960-62), which he was working on at the time of his tragically early death in 1962, at the age of 34, Klein took the concept of *Anthropometries* a stage further. Moving from the idea of 'figurative' painting to that of 'landscape' painting, Klein single-handedly overhauled, what had become a rather tired tradition. He took physical impressions of the ground, of grass, mud, stone and so on and then painted them blue, white or pink. These colours were of alchemical significance and derived from Klein's studies of hermetical philosophy. Klein had represented earth as an art object. Then, consistent with his cosmological interests, he went on to represent the three other elements. Using the same procedure which he had employed in *Anthropometries*, Klein exposed white canvases to the effects of rain, storm and fire. He had found a way of allowing the 'elements' to speak for themselves. Klein's *Cosmologies* demonstrated that the artist could listen to, and record, the textures of the world whilst avoiding the redundancies which were implicit in both 'abstraction' and conventional landscape painting. It is not difficult to see that Klein's resolutely 'conceptual' procedures were very similar, at a fundamental level, to those of the Barbizon school or the Impressionists. Like the works of those painters, the

Anthropometries and *Cosmogenies* of Klein are 'objects' of very considerable beauty. They could be described, loosely, as being 'ravishingly lovely'.

Klein re-created figurative and landscape art by exploring the nature of the human presence in the world and by redefining the way in which that presence and the basic 'elements' of nature could be 'represented'. The same could be said of the work of Robert Smithson. It could be argued that Smithson was a landscape artist. However, like Klein, he recreated the language of a whole tradition of thought about the relationship between man and nature. Smithson's work was rooted in a profound and extended philosophical meditation upon the classical trinity of man, nature and art. The starting point for Smithson's philosophical investigation into the language of art was his realisation, in the early 1960s, that an epochal revolution had occurred in the sciences during the twentieth century. Smithson was one of the first artists to explore the implications of such a revolution for the language of art. It was significant that Klein, like the early abstractionists Kandinsky, Malevich and Mondrian, was more concerned with mysticism, hermeticism, zen, theosophy, anthroposophy and alchemy than with the developments of contemporary science which had created the scientific revolution to which Smithson responded. Like his friend Don Judd, the writer William S. Burroughs and his exact contemporary Thomas Pynchon, Smithson recognised that the world which was being described by twentieth century science no longer bore any relation to the conventions and presuppositions of the naturalistic art which had been so dominant since the Renaissance. Smithson had made an extended visit to Italy, in particular Rome, in 1961-2 when he was re-evaluating all of his art ideas. It was after his return from the Old World of Italy that he began the researches and experiments in art language which were to continue until his death in 1973. The premise of all of Smithson's work between 1962 and 1973 was his belief that it was necessary to discover an entirely new art language in order to express, with any degree of adequacy, the world of sub-atomic physics, pulsars and DNA.

In pursuit of this end, Smithson chose to explore the ways in which nature, which he saw through the categories of economics, paleontology, geology and ecology, could be expressed in the language of art. Smithson interrogated the physical processes of nature. He researched the geological evolution of landscapes and habitats, the chemical and physical characteristics of minerals and the technological and economic impact of man through building, mining and pollution. Smithson's investigations did not result in the production of a simple object. He was dealing with processes, and sites, which were so huge and unwieldy that they could never be installed in a gallery or a museum. However, Smithson was not prepared to forgo the possibility of placing his findings into the public domain. He reworked the whole language of representation so that he could use the domain of art to exhibit his ideas and discoveries. This achievement is seen most clearly in two works: the *Non-Sites* of 1968 and the *Spiral Jetty* of 1970.

In the middle 1960s, Smithson conducted a series of investigations of sites in various parts of New Jersey and up-state New York. He was interested in their geological configuration and in the ways in which quarrying, road building and other excavations had affected them. He assembled an extensive documentation about these sites. This assemblage of information was comparable to the mass of impressions which a member of the Barbizon school might have accumulated during a sojourn in the Forest of Fontainebleau. However, unlike those painters, Smithson was not making an artifact. He was trying to grasp the thing itself – the land and the geology of New Jersey and up-state New York. However, if Smithson was to share this information, he needed to find a means of placing it in the space of a gallery or museum. His solution was elegant and challenging. He crated up a selection of rocks from each site and placed the crates in a gallery. Then he photographed each site and placed the photograph above the crate of rocks. Finally, he placed an ordnance survey map of the area above the photograph and pinned a market on the map to indicate the exact location of the site from which the rocks had been taken. These objects bore a close resemblance to the kind of 'art-works' which were being generated by 'conceptual' artists in New York and elsewhere at that time (1968). Indeed, Smithson's maps, photographs of sites and rather beautiful lumps of quartz, sandstone and granite, bore more resemblance to painting and sculpture than many other things which were claiming to be such. The greatest irony of Smithson's presentation was the fact that the finished gallery art-object was designated as a *Non-Site*. It was clear that reality lay elsewhere, beyond the artificial space of the gallery.

Smithson's *Non-Sites* subtly called into question the whole edifice of the 'art world'. The 'art world' was supposed to deal with accredited, real objects which could be bought and sold. In linguistic terms, Smithson's *Non-Sites* were a precise self-contradiction. They appeared to be what they were not. An 'art object' should, conventionally, have an ontological existence of its own. The *Non-Sites* had the appearance of such works, but in reality they were no more than signs pointing backwards to the sites of Smithson's investigations. It was obvious, to those who thought about it, that the *Non-Sites* were in the mainstream of the tradition of landscape art. It was equally clear that they were very peculiar objects indeed. They were, literally, 'anti-objects'. Smithson's masterpiece, the *Spiral Jetty* of 1970 was to have even more subversive implications for the conventional understanding of the art-object and its relation to nature.

In 1969-70, Smithson built a 'jetty' in the shape of a spiral, in a lake in Utah. He made a film of the building of the 'jetty' which contained a great deal of information about his reasons for undertaking its construction. These reasons were not aesthetic, although, as it happened, the *Spiral Jetty* was a thing of some considerable beauty. Smithson was concerned with evolution, palaeontology, chemistry, ecology and industrial pollution. The *Spiral Jetty*, and the process of its construction, contained information about all of these matters. It was built by dumping large quantities of rock into a lake. The rock was not indigenous to the locality. Such processes occur each day on building sites and are often described as pollution. The lake, in a particularly remote part of Utah, had a very specific and very unusual ecology. Smithson had been searching out such a place for a number of years. It was not an arbitrary site. The chemical constitution of the water, the plant life, the geology, the nature of the lake's formation, and so on, were all of considerable scientific interest. Finally, there was no way in which the *Spiral Jetty*, an obvious, and thoroughly attractive art object, could be shown in a gallery. It was rigidly site-specific. It could never be moved. Indeed, within two years, the natural forces at work in the lake had drowned the whole thing. Interestingly, in the years 1968-72, Merilyn Smith had also studied many of the subjects which absorbed Smithson's attention in the course of her work as a Ceramist. She had devoted particular attention to the geology of the land and seascape of Mull. In 1972, she had produced a work, *Mountain*, made from clay, which was progressively eroded by a steady play of water. *Mountain* was exhibited, in 1972, in the Ceramic Workshop. Like many of Smithson's works, it was concerned with the relationship between art, time, change and nature.) By 1972, *Spiral Jetty* had ceased to exist altogether. Very few people have seen the 'real' *Spiral Jetty*. And yet, this non-object became one of the most seminal art-works of the 1970s. To an even greater degree than was the case with the *Non-Sites*, Smithson succeeded, by means of, the *Spiral Jetty*, in subverting the whole idea of art as object. The *Spiral Jetty* exists only as an idea. It is extremely beautiful. It is packed with information about the nature of the world and the processes of nature and evolution. It touches politics, economics, ecology and science. Nothing more could be asked of any work of art.

Klein questioned the meaning of art, its objects and its language, from within the conventional structures of the art world. He made objects. He worked within the space of the gallery. It was not difficult for critics to place, or rather attempt to place, his work alongside that of the Dadaists, Duchamp, the Surrealists and the Nouveau Realistes. Smithson operated within the domain of the conventional American art world with its museums, galleries, art institutes and the rest. However, Smithson's apparent art-objects were not really objects at all. They pointed towards something which could never be contained within, or subsumed by, the art world. If that 'beyond' was ignored or discounted, then Smithson's objects ceased to be coherent. They depended, literally, upon the reality which existed outside the four walls of the museum or gallery.

Joseph Beuys' objects, drawings and actions premised upon an atavistic, and utterly idiosyncratic, language and philosophy were more problematic than those of Klein and Smithson. They were, quite simply, outside the current, but they were also art. Beuys, and others, designated them as such and paid the relevant bills, financial and critical, which were necessary to secure that status. Yet, for all of their perplexing strangeness, Beuys' most radical gesture was not the insertion of his bizarre 'objects' into galleries and museums. Beuys attempted to break out of the ghetto of the art world and take his art right into the heart of society.

It is widely believed that the shaman, so frequently invoked in Beuys' objects and actions, experienced no disjunction between his consciousness and that of nature. It has also been contended that the society of which the shaman was a part was, in some essential sense, more harmonious than that of the present day and that the gap between man and nature which has grown up since those paradisial days has widened dramatically since the Industrial Revolution. Like Klein and Smithson, Beuys was greatly concerned with this alienation. By means of his objects, drawings and actions, he attempted to remind the world of the harmony which had been lost and of the peril which that loss entailed. In order to extend the scope of his dialogue with, and critique of, society, Beuys devised a series of strategies for breaking down the barriers which had confined even Klein and Smithson to the impotence of the 'art world'. With his Free International University (1972–), *Honey Pump* (1977) and *7000 Oaks* (1982-6), Beuys broke out of the world of art and engaged directly with society. The Free International University is a peripatetic forum which concerns itself with a wide range of topics which include economics, democracy, education, technology, pollution, prisons, nuclear energy, human rights and banking. The presence of Beuys, who delivered long, poetic and enigmatic lectures about energy and society which he illustrated with drawings in chalk on blackboards, meant that the Free International University became a vehicle which was able to transmit the energy of Beuys' art into the more general arena of social debate and controversy.

Honey Pump [1977] was Beuys' contribution to Documenta in 1977. Honey, an ancient symbol of warmth and vitality, was pumped round a large loop of clear plastic tubing. The pumped honey was a metaphor for the flow of energy through society. Beuys' sculptures were often made from materials of warm energy such as fur, felt, fat and copper. *Honey Pump* also contained references to other works of Beuys. He placed small copper models of his *Eurasienstaff*, which had featured in a number of actions in the late 1960s, and of the three iron pots which he had used in the *Edinburgh Poor House* in 1974. Beuys also held a continuous session of the Free International University for the whole of Documenta. *Honey Pump*, in complete contrast with the open, pedagogical and controversialist form of the Free International University, was a remarkably dense concentration of symbolism and information. Resonances of important moments in the history of Beuys' activity as an artist were present in the details of *Honey Pump*. The copper *Eurasienstaff* was a representation of his shamanic works and actions of the 1960s. Beuys had used three iron pots in the act of homage to the Edinburgh Poorhouse which he had made in June 1974. The three diminutive copper pots of the *Honey Pump* were therefore a representation of sacred space. The large plastic loop, filled with golden honey, also defined space as something other than a geometrical quantity. Like the Edinburgh Poorhouse in June 1974, *Honey Pump* became, by the action of the artist, a 'temenos', or sacred enclosure. The linking of the current activities of the Free International University with *Honey Pump* completed the circle. The apparent simplicity of *Honey Pump* was a distillation of Beuys' complex and elusive artistic language.

The idea behind *7000 Oaks* (1982-86) was both simple and also beautifully resonant. Beuys proposed that 7000 oak saplings should be planted and a piece of granite laid at the foot of each sapling. This simplicity, like that of the *Spiral Jetty*, concealed a complex of meanings. In the first place, the oak was a traditional German, and Celtic, symbol. During the 1930s and 40s, it had been appropriated by the Nazis. Beuys' action, daringly, reappropriated that symbol for modern German society. Symbolically, Beuys was healing part of the wound which had crippled Germany in the years since 1945. The planting of oaks also had a direct relationship with the ideas of the Green movement in Germany. Beuys himself had once been a parliamentary candidate for Die Grunen. Many of the oaks were planted by individuals or as a result of the initiatives of small local groups. In this manner, Beuys' belief in participatory democracy was underlined. Despite such efforts, a great deal of money had to be found in order to complete the project. Beuys used his own position as a successful, very bankable, artist to raise a large part of the funds. He conducted auctions, sold multiples and appeared in advertisements for whisky on Japanese television. In these ways, the gross commercialisation of the art world of the 1980s was turned to creativity rather than into bank balances. By 1982, according to the lists drawn up by the late Dr. Willi Bongard, Beuys was the 'number one' artist, in commercial terms, in the world. The delicate resonances of *7000 Oaks* were underwritten by this fact.

7000 Oaks was concerned with ideas, with money and also with nature or landscape. *7000 Oaks* acted directly upon nature in a way that was thoroughly consistent with the shamanic notions which so appealed to Beuys. The planting of such a large number of trees was a significant modification of the landscape. However, in contrast to most works of man, be they industrial or artistic, the full shape of *7000 Oaks* will not be visible within the lifetimes of those who took part in the project. The ideas, the meaning and the shape of the completed work are not difficult to conceive, but as in the case of *Spiral Jetty*, the art-work itself is elusive, indeed invisible. Beuys was an artist who worked with ideas, philosophy and speculations. Without their illumination, Beuys' art amounts to little more than a detritus of fat, felt, fur and other bits and pieces.

The procedures of Klein, Smithson and Beuys bore a striking resemblance to those of scientific investigation. Like research scientists, these artists manipulated, and explored the implications of, ideas. Like the physicists who developed the theory of quantum mechanics, and so changed the face of physics, these artists made radical extensions to, and enhancements of, the language of the visual arts. Their work demonstrated that a visual artist could transcend the traditional categories of painting and sculpture in the same way that an astrophysicist could pass beyond those of Newton. *£1512* is a work which must be seen alongside those of Klein, Smithson and Beuys. Like Klein's *Le Vide* and *Anthopometries,* Smithson's *Non-Sites* and *Spiral Jetty*, and Beuys' *Honey Pump* and *7000 Oaks, £1512* is the result of radical enquiry into the nature of art and the conditions under which it is created.

The premise of *£1512* was the Ceramic Workshop. The Ceramic Workshop was intended to be a means whereby artists could break out of the vicious circle of commercialism, sponsorship and state control. From the outset, the Ceramic Workshop was organised as a vehicle which would make money serve art and artists rather than the other way round. The relationship between money and art is, arguably, a more fundamental issue than those explored by Klein, Smithson and Beuys.

By the late 1960s, when the Ceramic Workshop was first conceived, visual art had become little more than a means of commercial
exchange. It was, like gold, diamonds and commodity futures, a
medium for financial speculation. In phase with this process of
monetarisation, visual art lost the subversive, alienated role which it
had played during the nineteenth and early twentieth centuries. By
the 1970s, it was clear that 'avantgarde' had become a meaningless
category. Scandal and outrage were either redundant or else they
were immediately bankable. During the 1980s, these processes
continued, relentlessly. Advertising has appropriated, and exploited
without discrimination or mercy, all of the visual styles of the
twentieth century avant-garde. Futurist graphics, Surrealist fantasy
and New York School gestures have been reduced to the status of
arbitrary elements in the palette of the TV advertisement makers.
Visual artists, usually unemployed or chronically impoverished, are
deployed, as colourful extras, in government inner-city regeneration
schemes. Paintings, videos, posters, postcards and TV feature programmes are celebrated and merchandised up and down the High
Street. The visual arts have become little more than a series of chic-
nostalgic backcloths for a 'leisure' society. Trivialisation, stylistic
redundancy, pseudo-ideological posturing and simple hype have
overwhelmed the precision and intelligence which is necessary for the
creation of any coherent visual art work. Promiscuity had murdered
integrity. Money is the root of all art.

The survival of the Ceramic Workshop would have made a
significant contribution to the struggle against these dismal currents
of fashion and expediency. Had it survived the disaster of 1974, it
might well have borne comparison with the Free International
University. Its financial demise meant that its continued existence
would have to take a form which was more like the *Anthropometries*
of Klein or the *Spiral Jetty* of Smithson. As these works demonstrated,
the fact that the actual 'object' does not exist, or perhaps has never
existed, need not prevent the creation of a pattern of language or
material which resonates with the energy of its lost presence. Just as
Beuys' *Honey Pump* 'contained' many of his previous activities, so
£1512 'contains' the history and ideals of the Ceramic Workshop. In
a very literal sense, £1512 *is* the Ceramic Workshop. Its flourishing
enterprise had been collapsed, like a neutron star, into its basic
element – money.

A pulsar, a cosmological object discovered during the 1960s when
Klein, Smithson and Beuys were in their prime, is a neutron star.
Pulsars spin at incredible velocities, emitting huge quantities of
electromagnetic energy in the form of a regular radio signal which
travels distances of many light years. Like a pulsar, the energy which

was once the Ceramic Workshop will continue to produce a signal for a long time and over large distances. That signal is £1512. In 1977, the committee of the Ceramic Workshop invested the balance of £1,512 in Treasury Bonds. In 1987-8, the net assets of the Ceramic Workshop were £5,806. The value of £1512 will increase, very gradually, until well into the twenty first century when it will continue to grow exponentially. Like the 7000 Oaks of Beuys, the full impact of £1512 will not be felt until long after all of those who initiated it are dead and gone, but its implications can be grasped immediately. By investing the remaining balance of the Ceramic Workshop in such a way that its accumulation will never be drawn upon, the committee has created an investment which will eventually attain a value so great that the movement of its portfolio of stocks and bonds could, literally, shake the financial markets of the world. The policy of the committee is to invest in moderate yield, long term stock such as Treasury Bonds. With such a policy, there can be no quick returns, but the only eventuality which could prevent the eventual accumulation of a huge sum of investment capital would be a collapse in the value of government securities on a scale that would also entail 'the end of civilization as we have known it'. Such a catastrophe could take place, but assuming that it does not, the £1512 will, by the end of the twenty-first century, rank as the most potent art work in history. In 2087, for example, computer forecasts made in 1977 predict that it will be worth £1,600,000,000 (at current prices). What is more, its value will be doubling every five years. £1512 is a work of art which works like a legal and controllable computer virus whose power could enable the descendants and successors of the present committee of the Ceramic Workshop to control the global economy. If this happens, and there is no practical reason why it should not, then the late twentieth century monetarisation of the economy and the operation of the very traditional laws of compound interest will have enabled the Ceramic Workshop, in its incarnation as £1512, to achieve its original intention – art's mastery of money.

Icons were said to contain part of the glory of God. The Koran was said to be a literal aspect of the power of God. The Turin Shroud was said to have caught the image of Christ's face. £1512 is the essence of our mad society. It is money. It is also art. A kind of transubstantiation has been achieved. £1512 will achieve something which eluded Klein, Smithson and Beuys. For all of their resourcefulness, they all remained within the domain of art. £1512 has crossed over into the realm of money and thenceforth into that of power. Though no-one alive in 1989 will live to see its triumph, the success of £1512 is virtually certain. We know too much about the lethal nature of arithmetical and geometrical progressions to doubt the potency of processes which are determined by them. We are at their mercy. AIDS, the disintegration of the Ozone Layer, the destruction of the Amazonian basin, the Greenhouse Effect and the desertification of the Sahel all move to those rhythms. We should start preparing to live in a world where art has power as well as beauty and truth. It will be a novel experience.

The Ceramic Workshop and £1512 (Chronology 1970-88)

AUGUST 1 1970. Opening of the Ceramic Workshop in 15/16 Victoria Terrace, Edinburgh.

AUGUST 28 1971. Inaugural exhibition of the Ceramic Workshop Gallery.

1972-73. Invited artists worked in the Ceramic Workshop (Peter Blake, Ivor Abrahams, Paul Neagu, Graeme Murray, Nigel Hall, Ian Hamilton Finlay, Ainslie Yule, James Howie, Donald Hamilton Fraser, Herbert Dalwood).

Ceramic Workshop exhibitions in the Gardner Arts Centre Brighton and the Art Gallery and Museum Aberdeen.

Article about the Ceramic Workshop in *New Edinburgh Review*, 19, by Robbie Robertson.

AUGUST 18 1973. *Earth Images* by Ceramic Workshop artists (Peter Blake, Ivor Abrahams, Paul Neagu, Graeme Murray, Nigel Hall, Ainslie Yule, James Howie, Donald Hamilton Fraser, Herbert Dalwood, Merilyn Smith, Alan Smith)

Edinburgh Festival Exhibition at the Scottish National Gallery of Modern Art.

SUMMER 1974. Ceramic Workshop British representative at VII Biennale d'Arte della Ceramica Gubbio.

JUNE 15 1974. Clydesdale Bank gives Ceramic Workshop 11 days to clear its overdraft.

JUNE 26 1974. Ceramic Workshop grant application to Scottish Arts Council fails. Ceramic Workshop committee take decision to wind up business activities of the CW. Idea of '£1512' first discussed and agreed by the CW committee.

NOVEMBER 30 1974. Announcement of closure of Ceramic Workshop.

DECEMBER 1974. Controversy on letters page of the Scotsman about the closure of the Ceramic Workshop (contributions by, amongst others, Alexander Dunbar, Cordelia Oliver, Richard Demarco and the committee of the CW).

DECEMBER 7 1974. Federation of Scottish Artists formed after an open meeting of over thirty artists at the Drummond Hotel, Drummond Place, Edinburgh called by the Ceramic Workshop committee. A motion of 'no confidence' in the SAC was passed.

FEBRUARY 4 1977. First exhibition of *£1512* at Scottish National Gallery of Modern Art.

1978-82. *£1512* exhibited at the Kunsthalle Dusseldorf, the Centre Pompidou Paris, the Studio la Citta, Verona, the Murdoch Lothian Gallery Liverpool and other European centres.

SEPTEMBER 23 1988. *£1512* exhibited at the Society of Scottish Artists annual exhibition, Edinburgh.

The Blood of Lambs

Malcolm Green

AFTER THE SECOND world war came a reversion of the direction the arts had taken after the first: away from the 'sober' formalism of the twenties, which had shooed away Expressionism, to a new Abstraction which again looked for its roots in the unconscious. The painted image was seen as the direct emotional expression and accumulated energy of the painter who stood before his canvas. An explosion which soon raised fundamental questions about art and painting. In the midst of this international atmosphere at the end of the fifties, a similar about turn occurred in Vienna. Reappraisals of psychoanalysis, encounters with American art and a discourse with the Viennese fin de siècle bore the unlikely fruit of Viennese Actionism, which was to turn the Freudian teaching of sublimation and art on its head.

Actionism more or less spanned the ten years of the sixties, a period in which Günter Brus, Otto Muehl, Hermann Nitsch and Rudolph Schwarzkogler – concentrating now solely on the main protagonists who figure in *both* books discussed here – performed some 150 actions which shocked, fascinated and nauseated well beyond the borders of Austria. They caused major scandals, were fined, gaoled and forced into exile in Berlin, yet remained virtually ignored by the art critics of the day. While Muehl later drew his own consequences from the groups' striving for self-liberation and founded the post-Reichian AAO commune, and Schwarzkogler committed suicide, Brus and Nitsch have become artists with international reputations. Yet Actionism itself is generally more something that is talked about than understood, often being relegated to being nothing more than the Austrian form of anti-art, or the half-cousin of Happenings and Fluxus, or merely a belated Dada.

Despite a number of publications over the decades, with the exception of Nitsch (who is still active), it is virtually impossible to gain hard information about Actionism. However, something looking very much like a standard work has recently appeared: the catalogue to the exhibition 'Vienna 1960-1965' (which failed to be put on in Edinburgh in the winter of 1988-9), with a companion volume which accompanies a new touring exhibition. These two thick works cover Actionism from its very beginnings to the early seventies, and, thankfully, they are bilingual.

The artists all agree that Actionism had its beginnings in Abstract Expressionism or 'Tachism', where the painting became progressively divested of any representational purpose, recording instead the motions and emotions of the artist. However, the growing dissatisfactions with the possibilities of the easel painting and its limited ability to capture the subjective act led the young artists Brus, Muehl and Nitsch – at first more or less independently, then with increasing contact and collaboration – to extend the painting situation beyond its limits. The centre of the painting moved away from the canvas, started to encroach on life, subsume life, then using life as part of the painting until the canvas made way for reality and the painting per se disappeared.

The direction was first shown by Hermann Nitsch. In 1957, at the age of 19, he conceived his Orgies Mysteries Theatre which is to culminate in a still unrealized 6 day event, reflecting the Biblical myth of the creation. Its aim is to bring together the whole breadth of Western mythology and ritual in a Dionysian celebration of redemption through destruction. His encounter with American Abstract Expressionism two years later was a revelation because it showed the means for articulating his plans, which until then he had been searching for in literary forms. Placing the actual *process* of painting, in time, in the centre of his art, he saw that this self-hypnotic frenzy he entered was a direct channel to the unconscious. In the early sixties came the next step from easel painting, a form of 'action painting' where he poured colours, and later blood, over his canvases, gradually involving not merely actions but his actual body. But the real actions began with the incorporation of the eviscerated lamb, where the event, or reality, at last replaced the canvas.

At the bottom of this was, and still is, an awareness of the fundamentally synaesthetic nature of traditional painting: he saw that the act of painting the drops of blood in El Greco's *Ecce Homo* had been a mystic one, turning blood into paint: Rembrandt's 'Anatomy School' had similarly attempted to capture visceral, haptic reality with two dimensions. Nitsch reversed the equation and replaced the symbol with its reality, using real blood instead of oils, a real disembowelled lamb rather than Christ on the cross, reasserting the primacy of action over the symbol. He wanted to restore the thingness of the blood and nails of the crucifixion, create a theatre of actions which reveals the destruction myths of Dionysius, Adonis,

Oedipus, the Western iconography of cruelty, the ontology of the sacrifice, in its appalling reality, thus releasing the suppressed feelings of performer and spectator by a 'fundamental excess', his key (psychoanalytic) concept. He has remained true to this ideal, and all of his actions should be seen as excerpts from, or preparations for, his 6 day event, while his 'artistic production', which is exhibited in fashionable galleries and consists of the 'relics' from his actions (ceremonial clothing and blooded cloths), is its concordance. Yet despite the blessings of the state, the Vatican and the art world, his actions still provoke outcry and scandal, a fact which partly legitimates his theory.

In the early sixties Nitsch met up with Muehl and Brus (and later Schwarzkogler: the actual pattern of the growing relationships is complicated, but clearly illustrated in volume 1). These two artists had a more headlong confrontation with the problems of easel painting, attempting to break up and through the limits of the rectangular canvas with every means, slashing it, physically extending it, even urinating over it in emotional outbursts.

Otto Muehl's development can be briefly described as moving from the canvas to real materialism (junk sculptures which he also incorporated into the first public action, the 'Blood Organ' performed together with Nitsch (plus lamb), in 1962), and then from inanimate objects to live ones, then to 'material actions' where, instead of painting with colours, he painted with objects, combining a colourful repertoire of naked bodies, food, egg yolks, powder colours, mud, later excrement, and a lot of unnerving humour. He was now defocusing both body and object, both were on one ontological level, equal elements albeit in an art situation. But from here he could go on to take the important leap and create 'Direct Art', where the actions were no longer understood as art extending into and using real life, they *were* life in a direct form.

The actions became increasingly anarchic – lewd interventions into conventionally 'pornographic' situations, where not only was food denatured, repelling the obedient consumer, but naked bodies were de-pornographised. With the 'Direct Art' phase we see the Actionists at their most overtly political, tackling the bases of our repression, aggressively attacking the prevailing 'genital panic' and its role in upholding the state: the artists were no longer breaking through the canvas, rather breaking through societal and personal aggression, hypocrisy and taboos. The very bases of reality were taken to task, for as Muehl wrote: 'Reality does not exist, reality is fixed by the state. In the action it's up to me to determine reality ... and it's a different one.' By investigating the sources and nature of revulsion, the nature of the boundaries of one's body, the creation of social reality and the control of its definition, the actions not only tried to liberate, they also threw light on the self-destructive tendencies in art and man.

Brus' development was the longest, and most poignant. Alternately attacking and extending the painting in fits of intoxication and despair, he embraced more and more of his environment in his art until he, himself, came to be included, and with that he set out on his uniquely self-directed Actionism, starting with 'self-painting', a confrontation with the ambiguity of art creation which heralded the later developments where he attacked his body. Then, freeing himself in the mid-sixties from painterly considerations, he performed a number of 'Direct Art' actions, often with Muehl, finally to fix his attention on bodily existence in a series of solo actions whose intensity can scarcely be conveyed. These auto-investigations into pain and the body's 'hidden' functions, examining the presence and acceptability of the bodily self, culminated in Hari-kari like actions (e.g. 'Zerreissprobe'= 'endurance test') which questioned the whole validity of artistic expression in the face of the physical nature of the strait-jacket of societal repression. Brus' body became the revealed symbol of the controls imposed upon us by language and experience, and with chilling logic he turned full circle: from slashing the canvas, then incorporating himself into his art work, becoming the canvas and painting himself, to slashing this canvas and eliminating the final boundary between subject (artist) and object (art work). Straddling the subject-object split, he became an ontological non-sequitur, demonstrating the pre-linguistic tautology of 'I am body, therefore I am' and society's double bind. As such, the regressive, catatonic counterweight to Muehl's prelingual, deliberately childish demonstration of the 'unmentionable' side of the body, or Nitsch's voyages through self-loss and return to synaesthetic sensuality.

If Brus outlived his actions, turning to a voluptuous, subjective, figurative art, Schwarzkogler did not. Inspired rather by Arnulf Rainer and Yves Klein than Tachism, he moved from an early involvement in the Actionists' discussions and actions to perform six private actions of his own, dating from 1964. Often represented as the Apollonian pole of the Actionists, his actions were hermetic investigations into pain and castration, distillations of collective neuroses which he chose to overcome by drawing their subjective aesthetic consequences rather than re-enacting and breaking through them, overcoming the separation between self and other by creating a totally aestheticized, synaesthetic universe: a 'purgatory' or withdrawal treatment from the normal world around. His work ended with him demanding a perfection too great to be performed: he retreated into fasting and Eastern mysticism, leaving not only the carefully staged photographic documentation of his actions, but also a number of unrealized, exquisitely poetic scenarios.

And it is with just such artefacts – drawings, manifestos, sketches for often unperformable actions, photos, films etc. that the Actionists' development can be presented in catalogues and exhibitions, even if the Actionists' relationship to documentation was often ambivalent – a fact only hinted at in these two catalogues. Reading other sources, one finds very contradictory statements – from the initial enthusiasm about photographic documentation, followed by discussions of the negative or positive effects of the camera's presence (Brus even had to stop an action because the cameraman was a disturbance) and the film-makers own artistic conceptions, ending in questions about the fundamental veracity of such documentation. Nitsch could even reject film in an article: 'Why I don't make films' in 1970, and then sell videos of his actions a few years later.

Indeed, a number of ambiguities and contradictions have been rounded off, at the cost of a deeper grasp of the Actionists. Both volumes contain a wealth of lush photographic material and comprehensive chronologies – Dieter Schwarz's in volume 1 being particularly good and including lengthy extracts from personal diaries and notebooks. But an understanding of the chronological development of Actionism, while important, is two-dimensional if it is not accompanied by in-depth essays or interviews, and this is the major shortcoming of these books. The essays in volume 1 are, as we will see, missing, and the ones in volume 2 are either trivialising or too historifying. One is given a sense of saintly unity, for instance, in a group which had a lot of tensions and inconsistencies (inevitable when one considers the spectrum of personalities and actions – between Nitsch's liturgical remythologising of life, Muehl's devilish glee at degrading naked ladies in public, and the almost solipsist work of Brus and Schwarzkogler).

But it is possible that this weakness (indeed the overall hasty impression given by volume 2, with its unnecessary overlaps with its predecessor and sloppy editing) were the result of nervousness after what happened to volume 1, which fell to the censorship of two of the Actionists. Lengthy passages of the chronology were trimmed to suit Otto Muehl's version of reality, such that Mr Schwarz felt compelled to publish the unadulterated version privately, albeit only in German. The actual changes are not *so* serious, and some texts which were included on his insistence are an improvement. A close comparison even occasions mirth, for it seems that the Guru of the AAO commune has more hang-ups than befit one in his position: he cut out the Iron Cross he gained in the second world war, his waverings as he tried to break from easel art, and a planned piss-take of Nitsch, entitled 'Oedipus and his Grandmother'! But he also axed references to several important influences, namely a number of painters and the Actionists' early mentor and psychoanalyst, Josef Dvorak, who introduced Muehl to Dada and modern writers like Beckett. With this, Muehl has consciously strengthened the myth of the groups' autonomous genius.

More serious was the censoring of two articles, one analysing the Actionists in the light of Happenings – not necessarily to the Actionists' advantage – and, less understandably, another studying the Actionists in the light of the Viennese literary avant-garde. These interventions seem foolish because they remove the Actionists from their context. The intended comparison with the 'Vienna Group' writers, several of whom worked closely with the Actionists, would hopefully have highlighted vital aspects of the Actionists thinking. Indeed, with the lack of any proper analyses of their concepts (e.g. Dvorak's notion of 'Overcoming the Revulsion Barrier', Nitsch's Theory of Abreaction, the status of 'Direct Art' as reality, etc.) and their interactions with other artists/writers, press and public, not only does Actionism become remote, it becomes defused. While the first book gives a good idea of the group's birth pangs and gives good coverage of several early actions (e.g. the 'Blood Organ'), the second treats their major actions with kid gloves. Their intensity is hardly caught, a sad fact for readers who have not had the chance to visit the exhibitions and see the videos. Photographs may speak volumes, but the sheer power of Brus' 'Endurance Test', or the veritable lynch-mob atmosphere the actions provoked among press and readership, police and state psychiatrist, is missing.

Perhaps a clash of styles was involved here, between the Actionists' world in the 60's and the curator's in the late 80's. But something is seriously wrong when the last action in Vienna, 'Art in Revolution' (1968), which had serious repercussions (e.g. sentences of 6 months hard labour!), only receives one line of text and en passant mentions in the artists' chronologies (vol 2.). Not that a catalogue should just concentrate on scandals, but Actionism also meant fun, slapstick, fights, and inciting and involving the audience. And it is not mere voyeurism or nostalgia that makes one want to know why? what was it like? what they were up against? and what moved them? This desire remains unfulfilled.

So Viennese Actionism still lacks a standard work – something essential because their theories and actions still count among the most vivid, consequent paradigms for past and present problems and developments. Here we have a touchstone for everything from Artaud, Performance Art and Body Art, to Punk and Genesis P. Orridge, as well as writers like Bataille and the Vienna Group: 'with the shocking moment art refuses to be clothed in words and assimilated' (Actionist manifesto).

The two missing essays will be published in due course (bilingually). It would be exciting if this publication could be developed into a larger, perhaps less aesthetic concept, containing not only more essays, but complete manifestos, interviews and contemporary material which would convey more depth, more breadth, more intensity and more life. A direct book for direct art.

Books reviewed:

(i) *From Action Painting to Actionism, Vienna 1960-1965,* edited by Dieter Schwarz and Veit Loers, (under the auspices of, among others, the Scottish National Gallery of Modern Art) 357 pages incl. 180 pages of photos.

(ii) *Viennese Actionism 1960-1971,* edited by Hubert Klocker, 392 pages, incl. 262 pages of photos, being volumes 1 and 2 of *Viennese Actionism,* Ritter Verlag, Klagenfurt, Austria, 1988 and 1989.

(iii) *Aktionsmalerie – Aktionismus: Wien 1960-1965,* eine Chronologie, von D. Schwarz, Seedorn Verlag, Switzerland, (79 pages in German).

Further Reading: Any literature on the Actionists is scarce. The diligent might be able to find the two bi-lingual books which appeared in West Germany in 1969, containing manifestos, photos and scenarios: Hermann Nitsch: *Orgien Mysterien Theatre,* März Verlag, Darmstadt, W. Germany. Otto Muehl: *Mama und Papa,* Kohlkunstverlag, Frankfurt, W. Germany. In addition, *Wien, Bildkompendium Wiener Aktionismus und Film,* edited by P. Weibel & V. Export, Kohlkunstverlag, Frankfurt, 1970, although only in German, provides the rare book hunter with a large number of photos which have not been chosen with the art-historian's eye.

Autobiographies of Working Class Subjects

CHILDHOOD, CULTURE AND CLASS IN BRITAIN;
MARGARET MCMILLAN, 1860–1931 BY CAROLYN STEEDMAN (VIRAGO)

Lorna J. Waite

THE LIFE of Margaret McMillan is dislocated from the orthodox accounts of labour history. Carolyn Steedman's biographical project is to explore the reasons and effects of this dislocation by centring McMillan within a political culture and social class which makes sense of this historical absence. Margaret McMillan's name joins that of a list of many nineteenth century women whose lives are remembered in the twentieth century, if indeed they are at all, in a fragmented form which has filtered out a political and social framework in which wider aspects of their life and work can be interpreted. For instance, Charlotte Perkins Gilman is probably better known as the writer of *The Yellow Wallpaper*, a supreme work of fiction which explores bourgeois metaphors of female 'madness', than as a widely read economist whose *Women and Economics* is a classic feminist-socialist text. Steedman's account of Margaret McMillan's life allows us to hear her voice before it has passed through this filter, and in doing so restores McMillan to a position in which her class-consciousness and political struggle can be reconciled to her pioneering work in nursery education and in the development of educational policy at the turn of the century.

The social subjects who were the concerns of McMillan's educational and political practices were working class children. She lived through a time when the discourses about childhood were changing. During the nineteenth century, Steedman argues 'childhood came to be understood as an extension of the self: an extension in time, into the future, and an extension of depth and space, of individual interiority – a way of describing the place lying deep within the individual soul: always a lost place, but at the same time, *always there*'. Margaret McMillan gave meaning to this lost place by attempting to put it on a political agenda which affirmed its significance and transformed its relationship to existing theories of childhood, social justice and poverty at the turn of the century.

Steedman's purpose is to use the life of Margaret McMillan to illuminate 'ideas, ideologies, class and gender relations, and the social practices of a particular period of British history'. McMillan's economic and political activity was extensive. She was a socialist propagandist, a journalist, educationalist, theorist, public speaker. By performing these roles, she eschewed conforming to the limited expectations ascribed to women in the nineteenth century and offers new insight into possibilities for women's activity and the political structures which supported it in the years before women gained suffrage. McMillan's roles as an intellectual of the Independent Labour Party, member of three school boards in Bradford, teacher of adult education at the Labour Institute show some degree of power, or visibility in municipal affairs which was lost through the disenfranchisement of women in the 1902 Education Act and their exclusion from School Boards.

Margaret McMillan wrote 'if the voice of their own children – and the art of their own children, true, not imposed from without, but expressing feelings that have already been lived through – if this be ineffectual, then all the popular concerts, free art galleries and philanthropic entertainers can never hope to succeed.' For her, 'nothing stands against real culture, because real culture gives not only strength but the highest form of it. And this supreme gift is the condition, not the reward of victory. The people have to get it before they win, not afterwards.'

Her work, at a municipal and theoretical level, was to effect change in the bodies and minds of working class children which were starved of nurturance in a physical and mental way on account of poverty and deprivation. McMillan's emphasis on the body was informed by ideas from her philosophy of body/mind which had a place for working class physiological and cultural experience; starvation, emotional suffering, overcrowding, inequality.

Steedman describes the purpose of McMillan's words as trying to make available to working class men and women a metaphorical meaning of childhoods starved of a just equality and significance. It is McMillan's work in the slums of Bradford and London combined with her advocacy and practical commitment to nursery education which are her remembered achievements. What seems lost to historical reflection is the import of other forms of engagement by her – the public lecture, the prolific writing and fiction through which Margaret McMillan reconstructed her own childhood as well as that of working class children.

Carolyn Steedman explores the irony and indeed the paradox whereupon McMillan's icon-like image as that of 'caring woman rescuing working class children' in her biographies rests easily with an analysis of working class life in theories of education in the mid-twentieth century which disavowed any central importance to an analysis of political and social structures which did not project inferiority onto working class children. Using McMillan's life as a symbol, her biography juxtaposes literary criticism on the meaning of biography itself with an interpretation of the narratives of working class experience in which oppression and repression work differently for women and children.

A powerful construction of the life and times of Margaret McMillan is shaped by Steedman's scholarly work. She is a social historian concerned with class experience and the loss and absence of women's history from the struggles of historical explanation. In writing a panorama of the life of a central figure from the complex social and political configurations of the nineteenth and early twentieth century, she raises issues concerned with class consciousness. These have disappeared from the contemporary rhetoric of politics with its language and myths of a classless society of consuming producers.

Childhood, Culture and Class is a complex, demanding but vital book. Carolyn Steedman treats her subject with empathy and with a degree of conscientiousness which can admit tension, conflict and contemporary salience to its pages. At the present moment when exclusion of working class children from education, let alone an education which acknowledges the politics and psychology of a class-based subjectivity, is a fact, Carolyn Steedman's words and unique way of telling things, of showing us how class is distorted through the flow of history, is a biographical map of untold stories. Her previous books *Landscape For A Good Woman* and *The Tidy House*, in addition to *Childhood, Culture and Class*, are powerful and indeed poetic landmarks in histories of working class culture and its contested, absent meaning for women and children.

Sicilian Whispers

INTERVIEW WITH VINCENZO CONSOLO

Anne W. Mullen

'We Sicilians are born with our history engraved on us. Like the Neapolitans and the South Americans, our "reality" is so strong that our writing has to come from those very same roots. The greater the social unhappiness of a land, the more its writers are "vertical" because they need to explain their own suffering, they need to understand why.'

Vincenzo Consolo is a Sicilian novelist whose concern with the nature of Sicilian reality is reflected in his indefatigable recourse to events, characters and places in Sicily's past, both distant and more recent. When I spoke to him recently in his Milanese home, he spoke openly and at length about his departure from Sicily, his formation as a writer, and his writing. He had just returned from Sicily and the funeral of his close friend and 'master', Leonardo Sciascia.

His five works to date, three novels, one dialogue play and a collection of essays and short stories, although ostensibly quite different from one another, do share similar themes.

'In reality, all my books make up one book – a book about Sicily which concerns all the painful periods in its past and present and which is essentially the story of the defeat of reason.'

These are the words of Leonardo Sciascia and could be used to describe the narrative prose of Consolo. Consolo was born in Sant'Agata di Militello (province of Messina) in 1933; Sciascia in Racalmuto, 1921. The most striking difference between the two authors, despite their adherence to Reason and commitment to social and political justice, is Consolo's use of language. His hybridation of Italian and Sicilian dialects, purposefully using words which are philologically and historically meaningful, has resulted in him being compared to the pasticheur Carlo Emilio Gadda. Consolo's view of history is as polemical as Sciascia's although he has not adopted the moralist 'enquiry' genre so identifiable with Sciascia. Consolo uses the vicissitudes of Sicilian history to illustrate the melancholy and deep-rooted pessimism of the people. In addition to a sense of immobility, Consolo's Sicilian past is irretrievable. He strives to recapture, in detail, people, places, events and customs, so that one cannot fail to identify this with Consolo's own 'exile' from Sicily and with an almost atavistic need to seek solace through memory. One is always conscious of Consolo's commitment to his own art of writing, not just through his stylistic techniques, but through his concentrated effort to convey the notion that the ultimate truths of history and 'reality' can never be known. Writing, as an art form, is a means of escape from the essentially desperate nature of the human condition.

Consolo left his native Sicily in the early Fifties when he decided to study in Milan. When I met him recently I was able to ask him about his reasons for leaving and about his subsequent development as a writer.

You left Sicily to study law at the Catholic University in Milan in the early Fifties and after completing your degree, you decided to return. Then, in 1968, you once again came north and have been here ever since. Could you explain why you chose Milan and the impact it had on you?

Yes, I have had two 'Milanese' periods in my life. After finishing secondary school in Barcellona Pozzo di Gotto, I came to a sort of compromise with my father. He wanted me to study 'serious subjects' like industrial chemistry while I wanted to study literature. We met half way and I opted for law. I made the choice of Milan because I wanted to meet Vittorini and be part of the Italian literary scene. I hasten to add that I never met Vittorini – I was far too shy. I knew him from afar. My time in Milan was quite wonderful. This world I'd imagined through reading was very different in reality. Those were the years of post-war reconstruction and there were major changes. The foundations of our future country were being laid. The Catholic University was (and still is) in Piazza Sant'Ambrogio and in that square you also had the Centro d'orientamento degli emigrati, a reception centre for migrating workers and there was also the main barracks for the carabinieri police. This was the beginning of the massive emigration to the north, the transition from land to industry. Many were heading up to Germany, France, Switzerland and Belgium. The Sicilian sulphur miners, their own mines closed down, found work in the north. This Reception Centre attracted contractors from abroad who recruited for their mines here in Milan. The men had a medical check-up and then were suitably kitted out, lamp and all and set off. In Piazza Sant'Ambrogio we all met up: the students from the south, the migrating workers and most of the carabinieri in the barracks were from the south too. It was an incredible way to meet people from your own home town. We were the privileged ones. I came through university with those who are now the leading political figures in the country. It was during those years that I discovered what was to be my role in life. I learned to write.

After finishing university, I did my military service in Rome and then decided to return to Sicily. I wanted to be a writer in Sicily because in those days, to be a writer meant being a witness to an historical and social reality which was desperately unhappy and this was particularly true for Sicily which had always been so and still was. I went back home. I refused to be a lawyer because that meant being on the 'other side', the side of the rich and powerful and only the poorest people would find themselves in court. I didn't want to be on the 'other side'. I taught in the 'scuole agricole', the agriculture schools, and had to travel each day by train and bus. This way, I got to know the people I wanted to describe and represent in my writing. In those years, it was totally useless to teach children about agriculture: they were destined to emigrate. I tried to encourage those who had done hotel school to stay since tourism was beginning to take off.

You obviously witnessed some dramatic changes in Sicily which were then to influence your decision to return north. Your second Milanese period began in the late Sixties ...

It was 1968 and rather emblematically, January First when I arrived back in Milan that symbolic year. By that time, the peasant/agricultural world in Sicily was finished. The social structure left behind was one of clientalism, of Democrazia cristiana, Christian Democrat dominance. I was very troubled and anxious. I just didn't know what to do any more. I listened to the advice of Leonardo Sciascia and came to Milan. I decided to come and see at close hand this world in transformation, where southerners and above all Sicilian landworkers were flocking to become labourers and factory workers. Vittorini and Calvino, through literary magazines such as *Il Menabò*, which contained all these themes to do with industry, were encouraging other writers to come and see for themselves this world in transformation. So, I arrived in Milan at a crucial time of great social tensions. It was quite unfamiliar to me; I didn't even know the language, all the trade union and workers' jargon. I belonged to another world: I'd seen people fighting for land rights, for agricultural reforms; I'd seen them occupying that land to attain those rights. They had a different culture, a different language. Here in Milan I felt quite disorientated. Thirteen years passed before I wrote my second novel and this was because of this sense of bewilderment. I didn't know what to write about any more. Milan was a world to which I didn't belong. My world had disappeared and so, as a writer, as a living human being, I was going through a crisis.

You have spoken warmly about Leonardo Sciascia and he has obviously been very important for you as regards your writing.

Sciascia's first collection of essays, *Le parrocchie di Regalpetra*, *(Salt in the Wound)*, encouraged me to return to Sicily to be a writer. His work displayed that deep concern with history and its influences on the social/political structures of post-war Sicily, traditional elements of Sicilian literature. Up until then, my own reading of southern literature had focused on Carlo Levi – *Cristo si è fermato a Eboli (Christ stopped at Eboli)* and *Le parole sono pietre (Words are made of stone)*, the second one set in Sicily. When I read Sciascia's essays, I knew that Sciascia was not solely a master for me but that we were both 'companions going along the same difficult road'. When I was sending my first novel for publication, I sent him a copy and dedicated it to him. He had taught me who I was and what I had to do in life. To be a writer, the most important things are to know what you want to achieve and just who you are, have your own identity. Thus, Sciascia's work helped me understand what I wanted and what was to be my 'literary' field. I was not interested in 'pure' literature, existentialism. I wanted to represent an objective form of reality, always linked to history and so I entered into the Sicilian literary tradition which is 'realistic' and almost always confronts problems of an historical/social kind.

Before discussing the recurrent themes in your works, indeed the 'obligatory' themes of Sicilian literature, if such an adjective is suitable, can we discuss your individual works? Firstly, to what extent is April's Wound *an autobiographical work, given its time setting, Sicilian location and unusual form of Sicilian?*

It is an autobiography in the sense that it is an imagined one, a false one. I was just a boy at that time and I lived through those years after the collapse of Fascism. I imagined myself as being this only child of a widow but, in fact, there were eight of us and our father was very much alive. I suppose I wanted to create a different place. I wanted to portray the 'diversity' of life within an already existing 'diversity'. The san fratellani people of this north eastern town, whose dialect I use in almost all my works, are descendants of the Lombards who came down to Sicily with the Normans. They were mercenary troops who were part of the dowry of the wife of Roger the Norman. They came from the Po valley, from Lombardy and from Emilia, to help during the campaigns against the Arabs which lasted thirty years. Before even arriving in Sicily, some of the troops established themselves in Puglia and once the wars were over, the remaining troops were given land and chose places which were similar to their own up north. They settled in land and these 'isole lombarde', 'Lombard islands' remained very closed communities, with their own culture and traditions, and they were also linguistically distinct. One of these communities is San Fratello and its dialect makes an interesting linguistic/literary feature to study, within a social/historical context. For this reason, I draw attention to the suspicions it arouses in people who are outsiders, who consider it to be 'devilish speech'. It is linked to the idea of the unattainable truth of writing, a theme which is very much central to *The Smile of the Unknown Sailor*.

In The Smile of the Unknown Sailor, *the protagonist is the 'enlightened' baron Mandralisca who is quite unlike the noble antagonists in* April's Wound, *whom you portray as being in part responsible for the impoverishment and exploitation of the people throughout Sicily's history. The baron is different again; he came from a different class. You discovered him and his work and put together this fascinating novel.*

Mandralisca is more than a noble person. He is an intellectual going through a crisis. I discovered him in his different world of Cefalú. I used to go there with my father on the way to Palermo. Even as a child, I noticed that things were different from my own area which was more Byzantine. Cefalú, for me, was the gateway to the baroque world of Palermo. I noticed the changes as if they were part of some theatrical production and I had to discover more. Over time, I discovered Mandralisca's museum which had not been touched since his death and so I learned all about the man through his writing and his library. I was fascinated by the fact that he had brought Antonello da Messina's painting of the Unknown Sailor all the way from the island of Lipari and that on his death he had given everything he possessed to the people of Cefalú. Thus, around this historical figure, I created my own interpretation of events. I identified in the transporting of the painting the anxiety of an intellectual whose concern was history and learning from it. In the novel, each chapter begins with some description of the sea moving towards the shore. For me, this is nature moving towards history, history is being made. Antonello was an incredible painter; Messina was historically very rich but it was later wiped out by nature, by the earthquake: total destruction of all traces of its history. The portrait had been taken to Lipari which, although it was not terribly rich in historical terms, did exist. Then on to Cefalú. This journey from Messina to Cefalú is a metaphor for the passage from the world of existing to the world of history.

The most striking metaphor of The Smile of the Unknown Sailor *is that of the chiocciola, the snail. Through it you convey your notions of writing, of art.*

I often refer to writing as an imposture, as lies, as a form of deception, but a writer must always be acutely aware of, and bear witness to his own historical and social environment. I am convinced that the genre of the 'novel' is a hybrid. Firstly, there is a logical part, the prose, which has a communicative function and uses a linguistic code which is a result of a certain historical context because the writer is part of this and always returns to this. However, he has to be critical of his own society. Such criticism has to be different in order to subvert the linguistic code imposed by 'power', the national language. Secondly, there is an expressive part, a poetic part. In *Lunaria*, for example, the viceroy is critical of the power he does not want to represent, and so he temporarily loses his authoritarian voice and is able to communicate with the ordinary people in the village. Their language has many features of the san fratellano dialect. In *The Smile of the Unknown Sailor*, this dialect is the language of the prisoner who is condemned to death for stealing a lamb: because this language was his only means of communication which was incomprehensible and totally unacceptable to his captors, his own voice, in his own defence, is never heard. A similar fate befalls the peasants of Alcari Li Fusi. Their writings on the prison walls, which Mandralisca copies down in a snail like pattern, are similarly in dialect and are individual expressions of anguish and injustice which are never heard. These writings are the true narrator's voice, the consciousness of belonging to a certain historical 'reality'.

Your latest prose work, The Tombs of Pantalica, *is a collection of essays and short stories: fictitious accounts of rural life in post war Sicily, very personal recollections of those Sicilian writers/poets/ artists who have been important to you in your formation as a writer and essays on the desperate situation of Sicily today with the bloody violence of the Mafia, the senseless destruction of Sicily's cultural heritage, the Cruise missiles at Comiso. You carefully divide the text into three sections – Theatre, People, Events – and in the latter two sections, one is very conscious of a 'Vincenzo' narrator, especially in the People section wherein the Sicilian writers also become part of the fiction. Can you explain how you came to put together such a collection of writings which ostensibly seem quite diverse yet which are very closely linked?*

The idea for the book came to me while I was watching a Greek tragedy in Syracuse. I wanted to structure it like a theatrical production. The historical setting of the Theatre section provided me with emblematic figures who, as land workers and labourers, were watching their old way of life disintegrate. As for the 'characters' in the People section, I recognised part of myself in them. The ethnologist, Antonio Uccello, was a fascinating man who tried so desperately hard to save this disintegrating, rural society, turning his own home into a museum. Ignazio Buttitta is a wonderful dialect poet who literally 'sings' about that same rural society, while Lucio Piccolo was an extraordinary poet and he was an aristocrat, cousin of Tomasi di

Lampedusa. I have to say that both Piccolo and Sciascia have been my 'masters' and my friends. I found myself half way between them both. Piccolo was more from the east and so represented the lyrical, poetic side of our literature. Sciascia was more of a 'westerner', a writer of prose with a tremendous sense of civil justice, advocating Reason, always in the sense of the French Enlightenment. I was able to 'oscillate' between them both. It was through me that they eventually met, having respected each other's work for a considerable time. As for the Events section, Sicily today is a disaster ... the killings and bloodshed in Palermo ... it's a world made up of mad men.

The role of history in your works to date draws attention to the role of the 'intellectual', the crisis of the 'intellectual' in depicting the problems of those who are denied the chance to express themselves through writing. In addition to this, one can identify certain themes which recur in several works, for instance, the land theme which has continually surfaced in Sicilian literature. You make little distinction between the ferocity of the ordinary people's struggle for land rights at the time of the Risorgimento and the post war situation. Your descriptions are interchangeable.

The land theme is a crucial one. I learned from Giovanni Verga. In *April's Wound* and *The Smile of the Unknown Sailor*, I highlighted the problem of the labourers who were forced to work land that was not theirs. This was the massive problem caused by feudalism and the power of the baronial/landed classes, the reason for so much of Sicily's unhappiness throughout its history. History is always a disappointment; things you hope will change just remain the same. From the time of the Risorgimento, through the fascist era and after the Second World War, people have always clung on to that little hope that their lot will improve: they are always deluded. After the war, the agrarian reforms came too late because of the transition to an industrial society. In *The Tombs of Pantalica*, the story entitled *Filosofiana* depicts this ultimate irony. Parlagreco had finally got his little patch of land but he is destined to emigrate to find work. When he thinks he has found the tomb of Aeschylus, he has to rely on don Nánfara, the shrewd one who can read and write, who has to explain things to him. Parlagreco is naturally exploited. Yet another defeat for the underclass.

Your evocations of ancient Greek civilisation, mainly in Retable *and in selected essays in* The Tombs of Pantalica, *represent the futility of hankering after that seemingly perfect civilisation and on a deeper level, perhaps, suggest that the ultimate truths of all history are unattainable, that such perfection is illusory.*

I am very conscious of this Greek world and feel that I belong to it and to its Byzantine successor. Writers from western Sicily are less influenced by the Greeks because Arab civilisation subsequently had a stronger hold. In *The Tombs of Pantalica*, I highlight the destruction being done to Sicilian culture. I speak about a process of 'barbarisation' being committed against my land, my culture. In the last piece, *Memoriale di Basilio Archita*, I focus on this Greek matrix of our Sicilian culture. The collective assassination of the black stowaways at the hands of the Greek sailors who recite the verses of illustrious Greek poets at the moment of death, epitomises this process of 'barbarisation'. The sailors are so vainglorious of their Greek patrimony yet are capable of carrying out such atrocious crimes. These are the flaws and remnants of that same Greek culture which we inherited. This is the only piece I set outside Sicily: it takes place in the middle of the sea. It does not refer solely to Sicily.

You left Sicily in 1968 and do return but would you ever return there to live? As a Sicilian writer, what does Sicily mean to you today?

I miss Sicily. I feel a sense of exile yet, to be truthful, I'm scared to return. The Sicily of my childhood simply does not exist any more. It is a 'paradise lost'. There is only suffering and pain. Sicilian writers have always hoped for progress and they pay too high a price. Sciascia witnessed and chronicled this process of 'barbarisation': even when certain evils in our society are eradicated, greater ones, more terrible ones come along in their place. Sciascia has shown the loss of any sense of humanity and human dignity; total disrespect for all codes of behaviour. Sicilian writers are 'vertical' because their society is full of so much unhappiness and suffering which have to be explained. This notion comes from Moravia. I would prefer to live in a happier society rather than create happiness in literature but this cannot be. Sicilian literature has flourished more than any other regional literature and yet Sicily has become more horrendous, more barbaric, more painful. It is like some kind of cruel joke cast up by history. How we would much prefer to write about things other than our miserable society.

Milan
Nov, 1989

Note
The works of Vincenzo Consolo have not as yet been translated into English but have been translated into several languages, including French, Catalan and Dutch.

The Gentle Engineer

A PORTRAIT OF BURNS SINGER

James Russell Grant

Jimmy Singer turned up at Gilmorehill to study Arts, in the middle years of the Second World War; ash-blonde hair, silky and bobbed to his neck, looking like some Renaissance prince; though he had just stepped out of a close in Ruthven Street, off the Byres Road, where his family lived in an upstairs two-room flat. His face was pale and pinched, with high cheek-bones. His straight lips *pronounced* words, like they were giving birth to language; his long cadaverous fingers, much stained with nicotine, waved incongruously and incessantly to every word; his lean body, shifting in an ungainly lurch, merely a skeletal apparatus that followed his mind around.

With Polish Jewish Scottish blood (his father, a dreamer of wild schemes and a gambler), Jimmy was ambitious. Ambitious to write the terror and magnanimity and intellectual vision he had in him, which was vast.

We hit it off, almost immediately, when he borrowed five pounds from my lab fees; and paid it back, as he said he would, one week later. Thereafter, we shared the days and some of the nights, of our sojourn on The Hill.

After morning lectures, a saunter through the park to the coffee shop at Charing Cross, with news of last night's stand, – and fall, family troubles, our latest poems, laughs; then, into the Mitchell Library. Me, with a pile of tomes on Dante; Jimmy, wading into *The Ring And The Book*. Afternoons, taking it all apart in Brown's tearooms; and putting it together again that evening in The Griffin.

A night's firewatching, in the Arts Quad, or the Zoology building, provided the few shillings necessary for next day; while the blackout made the streets more intimate than sinister, the searchlights over the South Side and the Clydeside shipyards ferreted in the sky; and an occasional nervous gun stuttered, after the air-raid sirens went, warning of planes about. Stirrup pumps and buckets, behind sand-bagged walls, guarding live specimens in the Zoology Department, the warmest place there was, since heating was allowed there to keep the animals alive. In the pubs, interminable world-solving, word-dissolving discussions, with tipsy boilermakers and servicemen on leave, freaks and eccentrics from the Art School, and pale-faced girls, off the street, with nothing on beneath a plastic raincoat.

After two years, Jimmy abandoned the University to visit London, where he lived with the Epstein family; and later, moved to Marazion, in Cornwall, where he met and formed a bond with W. S. Graham. This was the London of Dylan Thomas and Soho metaphysics. War-weary and worldly-wise, there was little optimism about. He then spent time in Paris with the war's end, sleeping rough and selling newspapers. I had gone into the Army; and came back to finish my university course in the post-war years. By that time, Jimmy was back in Glasgow, and into science; his hair cut to stubble, like some dedicated rocket scientist.

In the smash-and-grab of peace, the entrepreneurial forces in every section of society, hard at work, and Scotland demobbed with no hint of national independence; the familiar power struggles of the ages went on to keep people from thinking about it, and preclude the possibility of any real change. 'They made a desert and they named it "Peace" (Tacitus).* The University had become an industrious hive where technical skills were taught.

Jimmy's mother had been ill in the Western Infirmary. She had pneumonia and went into a depression. She was allowed home on the understanding somebody would be there. Jimmy had to go to his zoology exam. He came back to find his mother dead, hanging in the bathroom. That same afternoon, as we were standing there, a letter slid under the door. It had a cheque for £100 (a hundred pounds) for Jimmy's poem, 'The Gentle Engineer', published in *Botteghe Oscure*, an international literary magazine, produced by an American, Principessa Caetani, in Rome. Jimmy made sure most of the money went to see to his mother's funeral, before his father got the rest. About two weeks later, we came in to find his father unconscious with his head in the kitchen gas oven. The ambulance took him away. He spent time in a sanatorium with T.B.

Jimmy was demented with grief and despair for weeks. There wasn't enough whisky in Scotland ... He would take a sudden run in front of a tram, if you didn't catch and hold him.

We spent afternoons at this time with Chris Grieve, in Hillhead. The wee cobbler held sway over sundry callers, while we argued the toss till dark. If was as if life was only an incident in the eternity in which we all lived. After some months, Jimmy went to Aberdeen to be with the fishing fleet – a period which produced the excellently-written prose book, *Living Silver*. His letters became more animated,

*Quoted in: 'To My Brother On His Sixteenth Birthday', Burns Singer.

full of his thoughts on poetry, his poverty, and rejection of any poetic criticism not in line with his own ideas.

We met in London, at G. S. Fraser's fortnightly Chelsea soirees. It was now the early fifties. All the London literati were to be found there, everybody who subsequently published. The senior members had mostly been in the Desert Army; and Cairo was their college. George Fraser has written an important book on criticism and he was accepted as the arbiter of what would be. With such influence, not lost on publishers, he was much sought after; and the eye-scratching and back-scratching that went on was ignominious, to say the least. Jimmy and I united in our contempt for 'The Movement', a group devoted to a kind of 'vers de société', the Oxbridge trend of the day. Jimmy's animosity led sometimes to aggressive personal confrontations, which left him with many enemies; but George and Paddy Fraser were unfailing in their understanding and support. An anthology of that time, which contained all of us, was put together by George Fraser and Iain Fletcher, and published by Peter Owen, in 1953.*

I went to live in Paris, on a plate of spaghetti a day. Alan Riddell, later editor of *Lines Review,* turned up at Rue Haxo (we'd never met), despatched by Jimmy Singer to ask what I was doing. The bits of a poetic drama lay in flimsy pieces round the room. In Existentialist Paris, wearing black and tartan, listening to hot jazz in Le Vieux Colombier, and students suiciding every night in the Seine, Simone Weil's book *L'Attente De Dieu* was followed by the first night of Beckett's *En Attendant Godot*; Alex Trocchi and Jane Lougee were publishing *Merlin*; Christopher Logue was into some mystical affiliation between the Knights of King Arthur and the Communist Party ... and it all seemed part of the same scene.

London was lit up with the Coronation; and George Fraser's literary caucus met in The King Lud, off Fleet Street, where the same scramble for places had more the atmosphere of a meat-market than an intellectual meeting place. Twice, I emigrated; once, in a boat to Sicily. Jimmy Singer came down for a day to Newhaven to wish us well.

When we next met, Jimmy was married and living in Holloway, London. Marie Battle, his American psychoanalyst wife, provided a warm supportive presence; despite which Jimmy went into the most profound melancholia, for which he told me he had been in hospital and had all kinds of treatment, including electric shocks. I was horrified at the change in him. We used to meet in pubs in Fleet Street and The Strand. He was a mask of himself. His whimsy and gentility had become a part he played. The panache had gone. His blank eyes

Springtime, G. S. Fraser and Iain Fletcher (Peter Owen, 1953).

were a mockery of the light that once blazed. Jimmy, defenceless, had stood up to the world. Psychiatry had done for him.

I think the aftermath of publication of a first book of poems is a dangerous time … We don't know quite what we expect, except that all that meaning and sweat must produce *something*. When nothing much happens at all, maybe one or two good reviews, among a flood of non-committal or negative reports, there's a strong sense of 'le néant', a black hole into which all our energy has poured. Jimmy had just published *Still And All*, at the same time as my own first book *Hyphens*. Literary politics are as shabby as most other politics. He was sensitive about what was said.

In 1964, he went off to do research in marine biology on the South Coast, hoping to regain his health; and one night died in his sleep. He was thirty-six years old. I saw the death certificate. There were no signs of any disease. The heart just stopped beating. That was all.

Jimmy Singer was unique in our time. His affinities were with Hopkins, Browning, Dylan Thomas, and Keats. I suppose he most resembled Shelley, in his arresting presence, his voracious intellectual habit, his air of 'possession', his attachment to the sea, sensuousness, toughness, talent, and ambition; although he made out he couldn't understand a word of Shelley. Perhaps, that was it. Life is too short for self-understanding too. The destructive and creative urge grapple together.

He was courteous and kind, except with fakes and pretenders, and in any question of poetic judgement. His interest was in sharing future intentions and the present moment. He never spoke of the past. The awkwardness with which he sometimes handled situations could be dissolved in a moment with extraordinary charm. His pride in his wife and marriage was plain to see. He never cultivated pathos. He could face the world on any terms like any true Glaswegian. When things were really bad, his empathy and tenderness were always there; he had a passion for living. Walking in the wind, with long strides, as though hurrying in case the scene would all melt away. The cost of his poetry, in terms of personal suffering, was immense. Apart from his chronic poverty, the disasters in his family, and the guilt he often felt stemming from his own wilfulness, he was conscious of being set apart, not only as a poet, away from men leading conventional gainful lives, but, as a poet among poets, he felt his separateness keenly, except for a few.

Jimmy's longer work is nearly all a series of epic similes about his death: for he had died, believed he had died, and knew it: part Orphean, part citizen of another world. Like MacDiarmid said of him, doubting … 'A visitor from outer space – not "a little green man" … There was nothing green about Singer at all.' Kilmeny gaed up the glen, and Jimmy, and maybe some of us; but none so persistently stayed there, and called back, rather than come to deliver their message. Always in deep trouble, always in Deep Space, Jimmy's signals were never frantic, but as technologically mastered as only he knew how. A language coded to give out distant vibrations ... so far out, they take time to reach us.

He himself emphasised this again and again. 'Break words with me.' (Sonnet III from *Sonnets For A Dying Man*). We have to interpret and we have to wonder. It's the wonder that Burns Singer was most concerned to convey.

NEW UKRAINIAN WRITING

EDITED BY
VOLODIMIR DIBROVA
R. A. JAMIESON

MYKOLA RYABCHUK
VASYL STUS
VASYL HOLOBORODKO
MYKOLA VOROBIOV
OLEH LYSHEHA
IHOR RIMARCHUK
OLEXANDER KUCHERUK
VOLODIMIR DIBROVA

Introduction: the Scottish Context

R. A. Jamieson

– A nation? says Bloom. A nation is the same people living in the same place
– By God, then, says Ned, laughing, if that's so I'm a nation for I'm living in the same place for the past five years.
So of course everyone had the laugh at Bloom and says he, trying to muck out of it:
– Or also living in different places.
– That covers my case, says Joe.
– What is your nation, if I may ask? says the citizen.
– Ireland, says Bloom. I was born here. Ireland. *

IN 1989, the Scottish Universities International Summer School (SUISS) in Edinburgh welcomed its first students from the Soviet Union. Among the group of four from Kiev, one of Edinburgh's twin cities, were Volodimir Dibrova and Mykola Ryabchuk. Their understanding of art and ideas, in particular literature, allied to the enthusiasm engendered by the novelty of a trip to 'The West', soon won them many friends.

In conversation with them, the parallels between the Ukrainian situation and the Scottish became plain: the imposing presence of the greater, not merely neighbouring but containing, political organisation; the cultural and linguistic imperialism of that force; the immensity of the struggle required to win the right to assert politically what is intuitively felt to be a separate identity; a common marginality within the European context – these were central themes in our discussions. Despite the obvious differences (the means by which the larger organisation has come to dominate through varying mixtures of the carrot and the stick, and the prominence in the debate of the Ukrainian language in comparison with Scots) much was shared.

The primary question continues to resonate: what is it that constitutes a nation? A set of written guidelines, a specific system of legislation, a fully integrated political organisation, enfolded in accompanying bureaucracy? A vital, native language? A geographical 'closed shop' defined by history, by a continuous line on a map, a flag, and the exclusion of outsiders? Or as Bloom might argue, a ground swell of a common feeling of belonging, uniting people regardless of race or religion, of language or personal history; a cultural (id)entity with no clear boundaries, but with a very real and open heart?

If we accept any one of these as a sufficient condition for national status, then both Ukraine and Scotland do exist as nations by Bloom's Law, despite the political organisations that contain them, and no matter how tightly they are squeezed they will continue to survive, because survival is essentially dependent on the land having some continuity of inhabitation and tradition, not on the prevailing political or economic conditions – though such factors will obviously influence its development. The particular world view of any culture is rooted firstly in its topography and its climate, though as society becomes increasingly urbanised, these differences are eroded, while peculiar social habits are accentuated. Yet even these are, in a continuous cultural tradition, rooted in locality, in the rural, agrarian community. And it is from these localities that we derive our first sense of who 'we' are – both personal and communal. In moving outwards from that point towards Bloom's universality, we must continually challenge our preconceptions regarding that 'we'. At best, a sense of identity is not a state of grace, conferred upon the insider by the progenitor of the line, but the springboard for a process whereby what lies 'inside' is externalised, so that people are less strange with one another; a process of 'growth', which is after all where the idea of 'culture' originates. Historically we may distinguish certain crucial events that have moulded our perceptions of who 'we' were, but here on the crest of the present, that 'we' is a thing in flux.

It is necessary, though, to append the broader questions – is survival enough? Should the conditions, political and otherwise, not be such as to enable that nation to thrive, to allow the process of change to continue free of external interference? In the past, perhaps ideally, yes. So we end up with enough material to keep the *National Geographic* publishing well into the next millennium. But this is not the way of the future. Interference is the only possible result of 'national', i.e. local, expansion. What we must try to ensure is that this 'interference' is harmonised and transformed to 'conference'; that it is not simply the swallowing of the weaker wave by the strong. And it may be that a nation's cultural identity, like the personal, is the kind of growth that requires a degree of adversity in order to develop resilience, a sort of cultural innoculation. It may seem paradoxical, but it might just be that a nation's culture continues to thrive and grow in spite of 'nationalism', which, in its good hearted but fallacious attempt to define the 'we', turns it into a museum piece.

All too often, we return home to our specific locality from the 'conference of ideas' wishing that more had been said, that more of what was said had been understood by more people. The sense of objectivity which we attain through stepping 'outside' our immediate situation into discussion with 'outsiders' can soon evaporate when 'inside' involvement and knowledge is required of us once again. It is often hard to communicate to those who were not there the significance of the experience. What follows is in part an attempt to communicate precisely that.

R. A. Jamieson
1990

*James Joyce: *Ulysses*; Episode 12: 'Cyclops'.

'We'll die not in Paris...'

NEW UKRAINIAN POETRY

Mykola Ryabchuk

IS IT WORTHWHILE to die in Paris? This question was asked at one of the first – and one of the most explosive – pro-perestroika meetings at the House of Poets in Kiev. It was raised after Natalka Bilotserkivets recited her poem, with the following epigraph from Cesar Vallejo: 'I will die in Paris on Thursday night'. So, the poet read:

> We'll die not in Paris
> This I now know for sure –
> But in a tear-and-sweat-soaked provincial bed.
> And no one will hand you your cognac,
> I know
> We won't be comforted by anyone's kiss
> The circles of darkness won't disappear under
>   Pont Mirabeau
> We cried too bitterly and overabused nature
> We loved excessively
> Thus shaming our lovers
> We wrote too many poems
> While disregarding the poets.
> Never.
> They won't let us die in Paris
> They'll encircle the water flowing under
>   Pont Mirabeau with heavy barricades.

It sounds preposterous, but the poet was forced to address this question quite literally, explaining that her reference to Paris had little to do with the actual city, where (as the Soviet media would have liked us to believe for so many years) the rich sip cognac and the unemployed and homeless die under bridges. She was speaking of the Paris of the mind – the Paris of the Arts, of culture, the Mecca artists visit in imaginary pilgrimages, if not in reality. In this context, it would be incorrect to contrast Paris literally to Kiev or any other place in the world. For Paris as a symbol contrasts sharply with any place where provincialism exists – even in Paris itself.

Why is provincialism, this psychological complex we so often raise in referring to our culture, such a characteristic feature of Ukrainian literature? There are a number of reasons. Perhaps foremost among them is the fact that there is probably no other large nation in the world about which so little is known. In addition, it would be difficult to find another country with such a small proportion of intelligentsia, an educated and creative elite that speaks the language of the people – Ukrainian, not Russian. This was perhaps the reason why Taras Shevchenko (1814-61), one of Ukraine's most renowned poets, at one point complained: Why do I write? For whom do I write? In a fit of temper he even wrote: 'Why in the name of hell do I waste my days, with this ink and paper?' Lesia Ukrainka (1871-1913) echoed these words, asking: 'How can I teach the indifferent to care? How can I awaken the mind that is asleep?'

Though it is important to note that these poets experienced very different frames of mind, nevertheless from the time of Shevchenko to the present day, Ukrainian poetry has been replete with themes reflecting the poet's haunting doubts. They feared that their work would be read by only a few contemporaries, that it would be forgotten.

'We will die in slavery', said one Ukrainian poet to those of her colleagues bitten by the 'Paris sickness'. Indeed, the provincialization of Ukraine, its land and its people, once so cultured, came as a result of three hundred years of Russian colonial policies. It began with a strict ban on the Ukrainian language and brought about the widespread assimilation of urban dwellers into Russian culture, with a concomitant growth of indifference among the rural population towards their national culture. The Ukrainian intelligentsia attempted a revival after the two Russian revolutions of 1905 and 1917, only to be all but completely eliminated themselves during the years of Stalinist rule. The artificial famine engineered in 1932 and 1933, which claimed the lives of millions of peasants, threatened the nation with extinction. Even today it is still poised precariously between life and death. The recent law granting Ukrainian the status of state language allied to a number of other measures designed to raise its prestige, have thus far failed to overcome the effects of such colonialism on the consciousness of the people.

Although the media has stopped speaking about Ukrainian language and culture as 'having no prospects for the future' or of being 'doomed', 'hopelessly provincial', and 'second rate', such views are still quite prevalent in society. To understand this, one need only look at the billboards in Crimean resorts, where films produced by the Kiev Dovzhenko Studio are passed off as productions by 'Mosfilm' (Moscow) in order to attract audiences; or visit a local bookstore and inquire whether there are any good books available. You may well get a reply along the lines of: 'Nope. Everything we have is in Ukrainian.'

This kind of situation cannot but have an effect on Ukrainian writers – even the most zealous 'aesthetes' among them, who live and work only for their art, must somehow come to terms with this. Some compose verses of 'repentance', for having sacrificed and adapted their style to suit the audience. Poet Iurii Andrukhovych challenges this practice, asking: 'did it make you feel better that you rhymed your lines in order to be understood and accepted?' Another poet, Ivan Malkovych, takes an openly didactic stance, in *A Village Teacher's Advice*:

> *Perhaps it's not the most crucial thing, but you, child,*
> *with your tiny little palms must protect that tiny candle –*
> *the letter i* *
> *and standing on tip-toes,*
> *hold up the crescent-like sickle of the letter ε,* *
> *cut out of the firmament along with its thread,*
> *Because, child, they say that our*
> *language is just like the nightingale's*
> *Though you should realise that there may come a time*
> *when even the smallest nightingale*
> *will not remember it.*
> *That's why you ought not to rely*
> *only on nightingales, child.*

* The letters i and ε distinguish the Ukrainian alphabet from the Russian one.

The very fact that poets are resorting now to such declarations seems to me symptomatic. After all, poets are not inclined to rhymed invectives, and are upbraided often enough by critics for their excessive use of metaphor, for their complexity, for ducking the issues and writing only for a narrow coterie. The cultural situation in Ukraine today is one that rules out the possibility of approaching art from a purely aesthetic point of view. Under present conditions, pure art is a luxury which writers simply cannot afford. The reasoning of those who wish to prevent young aesthetes from 'dying in Paris' is clear, but I think that it's unnecessary to put up any barricades to their creativity. The writers themselves exercise their own internal restraints, compelled by the feeling of responsibility they have for their nation's language and culture. 'We'll die not in Paris' is a single bitter, but fairly sober assessment of the situation our literature finds itself in today, and it opens the door to an awareness of our destiny.

Ultimately, though, how should the responsibility that people feel for their culture be expressed? By a continuation of traditions, hoping against hope to get the message across to the public at large? Or by the creation of a refined, exquisite, elitist culture, capable of surprising the whole world, and in doing so, attracting attention to a nation which does not exist on the map? Perhaps this feeling of responsibility should be expressed in an attempt to reconcile these two alternatives, to find a dialectic unity of these opposites? Contemporary Ukrainian poetry answers these questions in various ways.

On the one hand, there is a group of poets who place special emphasis on 'what' a poem is about, and less on how it is written. The credo of this school was captured most succinctly by Stanislav Chernilevs'ki, when he said: 'What really matters is not how beautiful, but how truthful, the language is.' Several years ago, this statement provoked quite a debate in literary circles and paralleled in intensity the debates of the past over statements advocating 'pure art'. On the other hand, there is another group of poets who seem indifferent to 'social problems' and are thus often criticised by the proponents of 'socially conscious art'.

These differences, however, rarely end in confrontation. This is partly because the 'aesthetes' show little inclination to engage in polemics, looking upon the others with an attitude of arrogant condescension, and partly because their opponents sense that they lack sincerity, that there is something of a pose in the position they hold. What is more, after the experience of the 1920s and 1930s, Ukrainian writers understand that such confrontations can be outrightly dangerous, as they can be exploited by outside forces. And finally, and perhaps most importantly, everyone understands that a diversity of styles is valuable, as it enables creative development both for the culture and for the individual.

Today, for the first time since the 1920s, we seem to have this diversity in Ukraine once again, not only within the official Writers' Union, which has evolved into quite a progressive organisation, making the issue of its dissolution for having been a Stalinist organisation in the past, obsolete. Diversity is also a feature of the 'informal' literary groups, such as 'Propala Hramata' in Kiev, 'Lugosad' in L'viv and the 'Bu-Ba-Bu' group of L'viv, Rivne, and Ivano-Frankivsk. These groups, unable to find their way to the reading public in official publications, compensate with skillful live performances. In addition, we might mention the informally published magazines *Literaturnyi iarmarok* in Kiev, and *Zhytnyi Rynok* in Zhytomyr.

Unlike the 'executed' renaissance Ukrainian culture experienced in the 1920s, that of the 1960s was merely a 'suffocated' one. Most Ukrainian poets survived the repression of those years both physically and spiritually. Even during the profound stagnation in the post-60s period, these poets continued to play a role in the cultural life of the country. Their work continued to circulate unofficially, influencing younger generations of poets in their formative years. So the continuity between generations was not disrupted as it had been in the past.

Today when reading the poems of Holoborodko, Kordun, Vorobiov, and Sachenko, it's difficult to detect the allegedly seditious content the government of the time read into these innocent metaphorical lines. It is difficult to comprehend just exactly what state principles these hermetic exercises had violated. It is impossible to justify the searches, the confiscations, the expulsions from universities, that mere possession of this material brought about. This kind of absurdity lies at the very heart of the totalitarian system. During Brezhnev's and Shcherbyts'kyi's rule, any form of independence and non-conformity was viewed as evidence of 'anti-social' revolt, and the unwillingness of literary people to conform to the spirit of Stalinism was viewed as an attempt to undermine the achievements of 'developed' socialism and interpreted as an act of 'sabotage'. This Ukrainian hermetic poetry of the late 1960s and the early 1980s played the same role in Ukrainian society during those years as Italian hermetic poetry played in Italy during the rule of Mussolini.

Yet however difficult the years of stagnation were for Ukraine, the country emerged from this period with its poetic tradition uninterrupted. Young poets of the 80s were able to draw, not only on the experience of the poets of the 1960s, but also on that of the poets of the post-60s era. They had access to the classics of our culture, as well as to the works of the Ukrainian avant-garde of the 1920s, which had been partially restored to Ukrainian culture during Kruschev's 'thaw'. They could draw not only on trends in Russian poetry, but also those in world poetry, which was extensively and well represented in *Vsesvit* magazine, under the editorship of Dmytro Pavlychko in the 1970s.

There is another factor of great importance that has a bearing on the development of Ukrainian literature, namely that we have a first generation of creative people who were born into urban families and/ or to families of intellectuals. These children were taught to appreciate the classics, to speak foreign languages, translate great works, and to view culture as a natural medium of expression. Respect for education was cultivated in this generation. Furthermore, this generation was capable of self-criticism, of irony – a quality Ukrainians seem to have lacked in the past. Young Ukrainians today have developed a burlesque-type of humour, which is the flip side of the coin to our pathos, our sentimentality, which seems to me to be a traditional aspect of our psyche.

The work of today's young poets betrays a familiarity with both world and Ukrainian culture. Yet no matter how new and diverse the poetry may be, it nonetheless springs from a certain national tradition, from a certain national mentality which has been moulded by a specific set of historical, social and cultural circumstances. One detects a common ideological framework in this body of work. In English, it could be defined by the notion of 'identity'. In Ukrainian, it should probably be seen as a search for both a national and an individual identity, a quest that takes place on many levels. This search includes complex ways of probing into the national psyche, through folklore, mythology, national metaphors and idioms, through specific national landscapes. There is perhaps no other poetry in the world that is quite so oriented on the past. There's a good reason for this. No other poetry is seeking justifications for its people's right to exist in quite the same way.

The degree to which a nation's fate is decided by the quality of its poetry is a delicate point. But if we accept T. S. Eliot's idea that poetry indirectly and imperceptibly influences the life of the nation by colouring the very nature of people's perceptions about the world, we can perhaps also accept another idea of his: that the loss of any language is the beginning of a decay, and leads to a people's inability to express the emotions they feel as civilised human beings. Eliot considered this a tragic loss for world culture.

Ukraine is making a valiant and inspired effort to prevent the impoverishment of world culture by the loss of yet another language – its own. If the vitality of the creative search taking place is any indication, it looks as if we may well be successful.

(A fuller version of this article on new Ukrainian poetry appeared in the Autumn-Winter 1989 issue of *Soviet Ukrainian Affairs*, under the same title.)

Some Ukrainian Poets

VASYL STUS (1938-1985) *began as a promising young writer and scholar, but was imprisoned in 1972 for his human rights activities. He died in a labour camp. In November 1989, his body was carried from a Mordovian (Russian) camp grave to Kiev. There was a huge demonstration, people standing along the streets holding lit candles, carrying yellow and blue national banners and tridents, the national emblem. Stus has become a kind of Ukrainian martyr. (Translations by Volodomir Dibrova/R. A. Jamieson).*

– Enough of bloodshed! – declared the executioner
When the knife he stabbed between my ribs
Was sticking out my back.
I suppressed the urge to moan and thought:
What if he would undertake to cure me?

Prapor magazine;. April 89

People
Doomed to death
Were given rifles
To honour their last wish
And they started shooting
Others doomed to death
In order to make peace
With their own impending end

Kiev magazine; Oct 89

How frightening it is to open up your heart to good ...
Frightening to concede that the human being
Has not yet died in us. Frightening to wait
To see when it dies in its hiding place

In the dark, to carry it inconspicuously
To the cemetery of souls. It's dreadful to be given after years of
    begging
Your strictly rationed piece of happiness
When it can heal no wounds anymore.
The bad is so tempting. How tempting is the sin –
To head for the Sun, pushed by the wind
so that one may exorcise one's self
like a bald devil. The crippled day
Will enter darkness, swiftly check the hiding places,
Hesitate because it's not worth starting the job:
A tribe of cannibals are sitting round the fire,
Yawning happily. Some meat
Is being grilled upon a spit. The water
Spills over the rim of a pot. They taste
The soup, meditate on philosophical antinomies
And discuss which one of them they should roast next
To have enough food both for breakfast and for lunch.
The crippled day turns back because the vicious fanged
Dusk will never creep into this cave
Until the last of these cannibals
Devours himself and is no longer
Wearing a proper philosophical expression
As if saying:
Life is short and there's not enough meat to go round.

Zhovten magazine; July 89

A poet of genius
Split himself /into himself and fear!/
Half a poet split itself
/into a quarter-poet and fear/.
A quarter-poet split itself
/into an eighth and fear/.
An eighth of a poet split itself
/into a pinch of snuff and fear/.
And now when he was walking along
There was a whitish smoke
Above his head
And scared passers by
Respectfully made way for him.

Kiev magazine; Oct 89

This ship was made of human bodies
Down to the last unit: the deck, the hold, the masts
And even the engine room.
They had additional trouble with the ship's skin –
It leaked especially hard in the sections
Assembled out of human heads.
When the pressure became unbearable
They stopped up the hole with someone from the crew
While the rest of them
Looked for a happy landing
Out in the open sea.

Kiev magazine; Oct 89

– Here's a sun for you – a man with a cockade on his service
cap
Took out a five kopek coin and showed it to us.
–And here's a road – he made several steps to the right
And drew the border line with the tip of his boot.
– Switch on tape recorders, radios, enjoy yourselves.
Take toy clappers,
Shake and beat them on each other's heads.
In order to to feel hunger or thirst,
Listen to lectures, watch popular films
About our future happy life
When you'll reach the promised land.
And to stop the rain from running down your necks
Remember
That every downpour
Will end sometime.
Even the Deluge.
If you get cold, sing these songs –
And he handed us a bunch of texts stamped
Allowed by Censorship for Choral Singing
By Two, Three Or More Singers.
– When you feel like having a rest
Learn to play an exciting war game,
Imagine you're surrounded by your enemies
Wanting to deprive you of your happiness.
So shoot, throw yourself at gun posts
fall under tanks.
Only – he added – *don't you try to run away –*

And we opened our loud voices and yelled in perfect harmony
 – *But Benefactor,*
  Who'd want to run away from paradise? –
While staring into eyes fixed underneath the cockade
That looked like two small drops of mercury.

Zhovten magazine; July 89

My Sweet lord, I have no anger or strong words
to curse my fate with. You take me
as a lump of damp raw clay
and puddle, knead with all Your fingers
to work up one more image from another
piece of Ukrainian soil. I knew life's soot
and lived through endless winter in Siberia
and I have grown a soul so transparent
that it throws no shadow.

Kiev magazine; Oct 89

VASYL HOLOBORODKO (1946–) *was hailed as a sixteen year old literary sensation in the early 60s, the hope of Ukrainian literature, despite publishing only a few poems. Then, with the end of the Kruschev thaw, he was expelled from University and returned to his native village in the east of the Ukraine, where he has worked as a labourer ever since. Holoborodko's first collection of poems did not appear in the Ukraine until as late as 1989, and even then with a limited circulation. But when it did appear, this collection proved that 25 years of silence had been most productive. (Translations by Volodimir Dibrova/R. A. Jamieson, from Vasyl Holoborodko:* Poetry in Ukrainian, *P.I.U.F. & Smoloskyp, Paris, Baltimore, 1970.)*

MEMORY

And an order was issued at last from 'up there'
allowing the growing of potatoes and other vegetables
in the cemetery grounds.
And there was universal clatter of spades, rakes and buckets in
    the streets
– people were rushing to claim the bits of land
for potatoes and other vegetables.
There was no good reason to do it though, for everyone
had relatives who were peacefully at rest there.
But they levelled the graves,
tore out irises and lilacs,
planted radishes and onions instead.
(Later they realised it wasn't profitable –
from morning till night they heard the sound of riders on their
    motorbikes
riding in to hold their boozy parties there –
at last they had plenty of fresh vegetables to go with their vodka)
The lines were straight and smooth
(tended like graves)
and people cursed their luck
at having few dead relatives
to feed the potatoes and other vegetables
growing on their graves.

THE SIGNS OF IMITATION

Beware at night and in the day when cherry trees are blooming
and when it
snows –
Beware.
Beware when sowing wheat grains and when you mow.
Beware.
Beware when deep down in the pits you mine
and when you draw those lines on canvas –
Beware.
Beware the coming of the no-man,
No-man will soon be coming to our land, be vigilant,
don't let him in and don't forget to tell
the whole world he has come.
No-man will plant trees upside down, will teach
birds to crawl, snakes to fly, will turn the rivers back,
will make them flow upstream, will dig great hollows where the
mountains
were –
People will think: *here's a real strong man that
has conquered the whole world.* But that will be a no-man
and soon he'll propagate himself and wipe out all authentic
people and
proclaim himself the only real man.
It will be hard to spot a no-man because he will resemble
outwardly
a man – he'll eat with a spoon and drink from a cup.
It's hard to tell what's in a wine glass till you drink it down.
Is it hard? Considering we all have glasses
in our hands and pour the drink right down our throats.
The drink turns me into a common fly resembling a bee.
But it's a fly. And who will then be able to tell a common fly
from a bee?

GETTING READY FOR A HOLIDAY

It's always on my mind – the coming day, a holiday that we're to
celebrate with spirits in the sky. I've ironed trousers, put on a new
white shirt and tied a tie around my fresh clean neck. I've asked my

Mother to bake a cake, to get apples and gherkins from the cellar, and I've gone out to invite my guests.

Now I'm strolling along with a friend and he's telling me stories from his work. And all this time the holiday is on my mind. We come into my room, he starts to sing a festive song. I walk up to the calendar on the wall to count how many days there are until the holiday. I see the day we're going to celebrate's already long past. I wonder why on earth has no one told me this, neither Mother nor my friend that I've invited round.

The festive Octobers and Mays,
Jubilees of deaths and birthdays
have trampled down much quieter grass
And what is even quieter than grass – the people.

They looked for flowers – handmade, and from nature born –
To bring them to the crematorium hall.
They put on proper trousers, ties,
To turn the wheel on, and on – in order to live.

They gave loud orders to parading masses:
Dress right, the people's pain!
Day and night they boasted on the radio
Of coffins filled ahead of time.

A Comsomol activist or a housewife,
Quick, catch up with your tail!
And keep you heads free of the grass –
Because that's the ultimate news.

THESE ARE TREASURES

Won't we see it coming in, this night,
the night that's lighter than days when we
eat our daily bread?
Let's not believe those who wear their hands as if
they are roots torn out of the earth,
those who are scared when their blood is stirred up
like sea waves – deep and vast enough to accommodate ships.
Their words are not true!

Because when we come back home we'll see
seeds to sow and a lit candle on the table
to work, to create.
And these are treasures.

* * * * * * * * * * * * * * * * * * * *

And then let the word die,
let everything that was spoken or written be forgotten.
Let radio sets and orators shut up,
and let the organs of lies – newspapers – stop issuing
and the libraries – these cemeteries
of dry, butterfly words –
let them burn down.
And then it'll be snowing in the woods,
and a man will walk out to meet his fellow man,
and a bird that lives in the white wood
will just fold its wings and chirp.
And that will be the good news.

While I was slaving at the problem:
Why does a pear have the form of a pear
and an apple the form of an apple
I heard somebody leading a horse at the other side of the wall.
I heard the rhythmic clockwork clatter of its hooves
and the dragging of the guider's boots.
He coughed – a smoker of tobacco, shag no doubt.
I had no idea what was going on there.
Are they about to butcher the horse?
Do they need it to steal away somebody's wife?
Are they going to fetch some firewood from somewhere?
Whatever way the horse was treading was pure maddening
  monotony,
Like a clock.
And I wondered: can it be a clock of some kind
Ticking behind the wall?
And then it dawned on me
Why a pear has a form of a pear,
And an apple – a form of an apple.

MYKOLA VOROBIOV (1941–) *began writing in his teens. His first book was published in 1985. He became a member of the Writers' Union in 1987, after some years working as a farm warden, a fireman and a caretaker. (Translations by Volodimir Dibrova).*

Traces of lost times,
Deeds of forgotten people
Summits and cavities –
Artist, watch out!

———

You said: come to me in winter,
I'll be waiting.
But how can one come in winter,
How can one wait in winter?
Neither you nor I will be there …

———

The ruins were dozing …
The sea was calling urgently
But the ruins were silent.
In the crevice of the cliffs
Out of reach of the bitter wind
There were snails,
But they didn't remember anything.

———

The night butterfly
Is not the one that is inseparable from the night.
The night butterfly
Is the one we've just caught.
We cannot make
A step away from this lamp.

———

When I first found in the depth of
The wood two wild apple trees,
They were staring at me
With hundreds of their pink and tender buds.
In two days
I went there again.
They were blossoming

and did not look at me anymore

———

The snow has covered all the roads.
Will the owner of white chrysanthemums come back?
This question has long been on my mind.
The dishonesty's inside me.

———

Maple tree logs
Are leaned against the wall –
Perfectly immortalised dreams ...
I thought somehow I'd manage
To live through this winter,
I'd survive somehow till spring.
But it is gnawing,
Gnawing away my old hut.
The hut-gnawer ...

———

THE BLUE CITY

In blue pipes
Everybody sleeps
Embracing himself,
Embracing herself.
The pipes are in the warehouse,
The warehouse is upon another
Warehouse
Of the city of the blue people.

———

An old man's sitting on the stumps.
Feet on the stumps.
Hands on the stumps.
He's sitting among the stumps.
And I, a small boy,
Am sneaking around behind him.
And he's telling me:
Grow, grow up
But not as tall
as these trees.

OLEH LYSHEHA (1949–) *published his first collection 1989; he is 'a quiet, melancholic, Zen-like follower of his own path'.(Translations by the author.)*

SONG 352

When you want to warm yourself up,
When you're dying to share a word with anybody,
When you badly need embers of anykind
Do not go to those tall trees –
You won't be understood there.
Their architecture is of perfect cosmic order
And transparent smoke winds out from their chimneys.
Do not come up to those high-rise mountains,
From the upper, one thousandth floor they could
Throw ash upon your head.
If you're looking for warmth
Better go to a snow-bound vegetable garden.
In its farthest corner you'll see
A lonely hut of a horse-radish ...
Yes, here it is, a poor hut of a horse-radish.
– Is there any light inside? – Yes, he's always at home.
Knock on the door of a horse-radish.
Knock on the door of his hut.
Knock and he'll let you in.

SONG 551

Until it's too late – knock with your head against the ice.
Until it's too dark –
Break through, pierce through,
You'll see a wonderful world.
It's quite a different thing with the carp –
It tends to plunge into the depth,
To escape into the lowest bottom.
Born to be caught, sooner or later ...
But you're human, aren't you? No one is able to catch you.
Carps – they are of a different breed –

For centuries their shoals,
Fearful and dark, proceed towards the lake bed,
They always move away in the opposite direction.
Look – isn't our century hurrying on, following them?
It caresses them with its own fin
And leaves them flat.
But you're human, aren't you?
Don't give up – break, push, kick!
Until it's too late – knock with your head against the ice ...
Oh, what a wonderful, boundless, snowy world!

IHOR RIMARCHUK (1958–) *is one of the so-called 'happier' new generation of poets, one of the leaders of the new 'metaphorical' stream in Ukrainian poetry.*

SIGN

I have flown through a hundred worlds as one,
I have made a hundred shoulders bleed against the sky,
I have fallen into the dark embrace of blackberries
When the Mother called me to come to her.

But when to the earth's essence
I pressed my swollen body
The grass pointed with a sharp finger
to the purple sun high above.

Molod magazine; 1988

STAR

I would, probably, live in an invisible way –
But on one July night
A star has fallen from above
Into a child's open eyes.

It has scorched a furrow between brows
And sown the memory with ashes ...
I wanted to wipe it off –
But my palm was too small.

Molod magazine; 1988

IT HAS BEEN RAINING FOR SO LONG

It has been raining for so long
    As if it hopes to wash away
    ages-long memories and traces on stones,
a mushroom is still sprouting,
    pushing away last year's leaves –
    it's stirring ...
    let it stir – don't cut it,
the word is still growing pale,
    it's irresolute, like steel on a wrist,
    for the earth is still so fertile,
    as if it was pronounced by a poet,
There will still be a great feast,
    faraway travel, hospital flowers –
    and there was heraldry with a golden mane,
    there was unread youth,
    there was everything ...
    you said so? you said?

And now, brother, go:
the snows are close.

Molod magazine; 1988

OLEXANDER KUCHERUK

KIEV: SPRING DAGUERREOTYPE

The emerging sun
Claws with soft paws
at the necks of passers-by
And they take their hats off
Greeting
The appearance of Spring,
Without suspecting
Its disgraceful end.
Because nobody will remember
What was written in the newspapers
a month ago
Surprised by the attack of warmth
and by queues for ice-cream.
But the Spring, like the local train,
Will go begging,
Making everybody
Who remembers its wonderful emergence
Bend their heads.

KIEV: WINTER DAGUERREOTYPE

It's not a dream – it's Winter now.
The city surrenders at the falling of snow.
Without torment
Nothing casts a shadow, the lonely sounds
On the white background
The height entangled itself in the white wires
The trams having got off their tracks
Make up new timetables.
Where's up, where's down? The confused policeman
Will give no answer.
Bullfinch-kisses fly from girls' lips
Missing those for whom they were intended –
They vanish singing like the echo in the underground.

The white people hurry, white cars run.
My skin is feeling that I'm in the middle of the day,
Everybody's waiting for something, but nobody's saying a
    word
About it.
Towards evening the roofs become dark, gradually from
    weathercock
and chimney, along the pipes, enveloping windows, balconies,
flowing down along the black passages to the underground
    tunnels,
Mixing with the smell of coffee, cigarette smoke and
Cheap powder.
The yellow light of lanterns catches people,
some rushing to their children, tv sets, and empty rooms,
worthless souvenirs and dust on books – they are hurrying
    home.
The solitary birds are hiding in the wrinkles of the houses.
The last passers-by disappear in the black hole of a warm
    doorway.
The day has recoiled.
It's not a dream – it's winter already.

MYKOLA RYABCHUK (1953–) *is a leading member of the Writers' Union in Kiev, critic and senior editor of* Vsesvit (Universe), *a magazine of world literature. In 1989, his own first collection of poetry was published. The following poems are taken from a poem sequence,* The Straightforward Poems. *(Translated by Mykola Ryabchuk/R. A. Jamieson).*

1.

here I am
my dear poets
setting about poetry

oh yes
I also
fall for this ancient deception
and so
I try to warm
the frozen birds

to part
the tatty pigeon's wings

maybe something will change
the wind will rise
the wings will spread
and the sawdust won't sprinkle
and those glass eyes
may blink

2.

war is kill-or cure-all
for poverty, idleness
famine

against AIDS
plague
cancer

the deathrate of the young

and the deathrate of the old

the number of the wounded
in the triumphant war
is minimal

the number of those killed
does not exceed
the whole population

but the essence of war is this:
on the battlefield
everyone can be
Napoleon
Caesar
Alexander

without risking
getting locked up

4.

three boys
are carrying their wounded playmate
with pistols pushed under their belts

– you're killed! –
the wounded one is crying
and tries to tear himself away
– you're killed! –

but killed don't hear

killed always
don't hear

5.

this worker
from the locomotive repair yard
who has bravely climbed the wall
crossed the frozen puddles

run to the paper kiosk
now asks the first issue of your magazine
why

yes yes why
what's in it for me?
you are looking through its contents
shifting assumptions

damned intelligent
prattle
scribbler

6.

we have been trained to write
about everything on earth
from Fujiyama Long Island
Loch Ness

about the nuclear processes
metaphysical speculation
eutrophy eclectia
explosions

perception and reception
extrasensory infrastructurity
gnoseology agnosticism

now it would be right
if we could learn
to write nothing
when

when half a kingdom is exchanged for a poem
and half –
for a piece of clean paper

9.

verses are always
'free'

even if
we rhymed them
put them in irons
imprisoned them in folios

they'd still behave like the fox
which played possum
on the fresh snow

so let's not kid ourselves
the fox will spring to life again
snow will stay white
paper empty

11.

life goes
crawls
creeps over

from one place to another
like tortoise
or hedgehog

draws its head in
tail
paws

so that we
when colliding with quills
hitting our foreheads against the shell
think:

life goes
burning our fingers
foreheads
souls

meanwhile its lying
at our feet
curled up in a ball

Why don't we do it in the road?

FROM 'THE BEATLES SONGBOOK'

Volodimir Dibrova

No one's really watching us
Why don't we do it in the road?

I WOKE UP at seven and looked out the window.

The beginning of a new day was so dazzling that I had to turn my back to my hotel roommates and cross myself. The cross I made turned out to be a very squint one due to my lack of practice.

A couple of days before the end of the summer term I had been given a book about Dostoyevsky in which the word *God* was written with a capital letter. I was to return it next morning and not show it to anybody. The book was published in Paris and the author was Berdyayev. I worked out a summary of it and made a point of clearing up all this business about God.

The truck drivers had already gone. They would have left at five in order to clock up their four hundred kilometres before it got too hot. I scavenged the lard and tomatoes they had left on the breakfast table, got my passport from the hotel clerk and headed out to hitch a lift.

The cheeky young sun was climbing towards the top of the sky. I marched down the road singing the folk song '*Green Hop*'. Then having warmed my voice up on this, I broke into the Beatles' '*Why don't we do it in the road?*'

– No one's really watching us – I shouted – why don't we do it in the road?

Three years University are behind me, two still to go. I've had my exams and now I'm heading down towards the sea and couldn't give a damn about anything. I can see my long awaited freedom, lucid, transparent, eating a full meal from morning air and heavy haystack yellow.

Why the hell can't we now and always live like this? Are we not able to? Don't people want to? Are we afraid? Afraid of what? But wait a minute, if the soul is really immortal, then ...

A lorry stopped to give me a ride and the driver gets a story of how a poor student of archeology got lost on his way to the dig and is now trying to catch up with the group.

He took me to a small town and pulled in. I thanked him and carried on walking.

At the bottom of the hill there was a police patrol. A sergeant stuck his arm out of the window and beckoned me over.

– Where are you from?

I told him. He looked surprised and swore.

– Copulate me! Where are you heading to?

I told him. He asked to see my papers.

– So you're hitching, eh? – he flicked through my passport – Why is your home address entered on the page before the date of issue?

The state borders were far away, I had well pressed trousers on, I had done nothing, so when he told me to get into the car, I didn't object, just asked him if he would please drive me back to the highway later.

The sergeant took me to the senior lieutenant's office on the first floor of the local police station. The senior lieutenant opened my passport, addressed me by my first and patronymic names and asked me to tell him what I was doing in his district.

It was useless if not dangerous to try to deceive him so I told the truth: I'm hitching down south to the sea, simple as that.

– Why didn't you take a train?

– I have no money.

– Why are you going if you have no money?

– I have enough for my food.

The lieutenant didn't believe me and advised me not to lie to him because he could easily check up.

– We'll keep you in – he said – until we have the truth.

I remembered that in the Crimea my artist friends were living somewhere in tents near Theodosia.

– I'm going to join them so that I can learn to be a painter.

– Why can't you learn to paint at home? – he didn't wait for a reply – Come on. Let's see what you've got in your rucksack.

I took out a packet containing soup, toothpaste, then a sleeping bag and various artistic paraphernalia wrapped in cellophane: water-colours, a notebook, and a collection of Rilke's poetry.

– So far you see I haven't drawn or painted anything but hopefully...

– Wait a minute – he started – What's this?

He fished out several sheets of paper from a cardboard file. These were Xerox copies of some pages from a book of Osip Mandelstam's prose. The woman who had secretly made them for me wasn't careful enough and had run off extra copies. I had taken them to make notes on, or use as toilet paper.

– Photocopies! – The eyes of the senior lieutenant flashed and he fell to reading avidly.

On the first sheet there was a title 'Mensheviks in Georgia' and the name of a German politician, Kautsky. On the second and third were extracts from 'Journey to Armenia', four pages of poet's prose broken into uneven paragraphs. On the fourth sheet, a commentary which began with the words 'philosopher-mystic Leontyev, largely misunderstood by his contemporaries' and ended with 'numerous manifestos'.

– Where did you get this from? – The lieutenant was a handsome young man, thin and tanned, with clever suspicious eyes. He obviously attended refresher courses and knew what a dangerous thing a copier was.

– It's my toilet paper.

– I am asking where you got it from.

– I found it.

– Where?

– Near the cinema, you know, next to the bookbinder's shop.

– What were you doing there?

– I was ordering the cover for my project.

– Project?

– Of the course.

– Of what course?

– Of the third-year course.

– Were you given these sheets at the bookbinder's shop?

– I told you I found them.

– At the shop?

– No, outside the shop.

– In the street?

– No, let me draw you a diagram.

To stop it from trembling I held the pen tight with all my fingers and started drawing an intricate diagram of the back yard, illustrating the many passages, the exchange point for empty bottles and jars, slippery stairs and the rubbish skip alive with dirty pigeons, where on the such and such of May this year, or to be exact the such and such of June, this year of course, I, having left the bookbinder's shop, was looking for some paper to wrap my course project in when I happened to come across these sheets of paper which attracted my attention but I haven't read them, not so much as a glance, I only took them as I thought they'd come in handy...

The lieutenant used the phone. A tall stern officer who looked like a B-movie star came into the room.

– A touring actor, eh? – He nudged the lieutenant.

– A courier – replied the lieutenant, spreading the material evidence out neatly on the table, – carrying a shipment of illegal literature.

The tall officer picked up some sheets and started to examine them. His forehead rippled like the sand on the shore. Of all the printed words he seemed to understand only two – 'Mensheviks' and 'Georgia'.

– And what's he got in the sack?

The senior lieutenant ordered me to show him all my books and notebooks.

– What's that there?

– That's well you know it's just my writing pad, I mean I'm not a writer, I'm still a student, I just jot down anything of interest that takes my fancy, you know ... here have a look ...

I thrust my fingers deep into the notebook, twisting the pages over, turning them from the one side to another so that the police would not see the banned surnames of Hrushevsky and Yefremov among the Beatles' lyrics.

– Here have a look – I said again, and pointed to the 'acceptable' poems of Vorobiov and Kostenko.

– OK. – I closed the notebook, feeling enormous relief. At the end of it was the detailed summary of Berdyayev's work in which *God* was written with a capital letter.

– So what do we do with him? – the senior lieutenant asked his superior.

– Call them. Let them decide.

The B-movie star wrote the number on the desk pad, then told me to follow him downstairs.

– Just leave your things here.

I was shown into the room where the lower ranking policemen dealt with everyday matters, the domestic squabbles and the drunks. There was a tattered map of the district pinned to the wall, and alongside it a copy of the local police bulletin.

While the sharp eyed lieutenant upstairs was dialling Their number, I figured out the reason why we don't do it in the road. But I couldn't get my head together and my heart was trying to bang away a whole life's quota of beats, like it was racing towards a final rest.

The policeman hauled in an old dosser who had been caught napping in the park, another man was showing his bruised head as evidence of an assault by a neighbour, a woman whose daughter had run away from home was wailing while I was murmuring – Jesus Christ – then again – Jesus Christ – then – have mercy on me. This prayer I had copied out from a book published not in Paris this time, but in St. Petersburg.

What could they do to me for Mandelstam? Nothing. The main thing here is that this expert they're calling in doesn't snoop out *God* in my notebook. If he does, nothing will help me. Expulsion from the University would be the lowest price I'd have to pay. I make up my mind to stay cool, polite but not too zealous. Yes, I did find Mandelstam, but I haven't the faintest idea what it really is. Yes, I have made a synopsis of Berdyayev's book because I was foolish and interested in all kinds of rubbish. The book was given to me by a Jew who shortly afterwards emigrated to Israel. I have never shown my notes to anybody or even read them through myself.

Jesus Christ have mercy on me!

The shaggy old man who has been caught sleeping on the grass asks permission to smoke, then suddenly takes off, heading for the door. He is grabbed and thrown into a cell, where he is beaten. O Jesus Christ! They chuck him out again, he gives everyone a huge wink and rolls a cigarette. They shout at him, why you dog's sexual organ you, haven't you been beaten enough already? Have mercy on me!

The old man is very soft, his eyes are clouded with mist, some sort of liquid is running down his trouser leg – have mercy on me, Jesus Christ! They beat him right in front of everyone. The duty officer, a junior lieutenant, begins his official report.

– Your surname! he demands.

– A man! – the old guy snaps, with dignity.

The lieutenant is genuinely surprised for a moment, then mocks him:

– Call yourself a man? Look at you! You're covered in puke, you've pissed yourself.

The dosser is dumped back in the cell. I'm ordered to go upstairs to the first floor. A sergeant escorts me. Before entering the room, I manage to cross myself three times.

The senior lieutenant is with a small fat man in a suit. He inquires where I got the photocopies from and I repeat the story about the bookbinder's shop and the yard with the skip and the pigeons.

The fat man is silent. I know he has my name and all my passport details recorded in his notebook.

– Sign here please.

The senior lieutenant hands me a protocol report. It reads that I am hitching down to the Crimea to meet up with an artist friend ... Jesus Christ have mercy on me ... in order to learn to paint.

I sign it.

– Show him down – the senior lieutenant instructs the sergeant – and take the rucksack with you.

Haven't they read the notebook? Didn't they understand what's written there? Who is that fat man? What if he isn't the one they're waiting for but just a visitor or something?

Thank you Jesus Christ, thanks a million, I'm whispering all the way down. It's vitally important now to tear at least one page out of my notebook, at least a piece of it, the title of the book. If they don't recognise Berdyayev, then Mandelstam alone won't get me into trouble. I only found it and I'm going to wipe my arse with it, you know how it is, we're all human beings, we've all got to go. Jesus Christ, have mercy on me.

Two hulking policemen are pulling in an emaciated man with strange whitish eyes. He tries to make idle chat but the junior lieutenant interrupts. Whatever he's done, he has to be punished. Kicked. It wouldn't be right to pass him over, maybe even a sin.

– Who are you?

– Nechuparellolenyky...

– Listen, urine bag, male sexual organ, you'd better stop fooling around and tell me who you think you are that can go walking about without papers.

Now I've got to somehow invisibly undo the rucksack, find the bundle, take out the notebook, carefully tear out the page ... and eat it!

– Give me your name, you copulating canine!

The drunk stands to attention and reports.

– Nechuparellolenyky.

– Nechuparello can go and stick his member in his hearing organ! Your name!

– Ne .. chy .. po .. ren. . ko – Leo .. nyd – My .. ky .. to .. vych – the drunk introduces himself accenting each syllable, clicks his heels, tries to stand up straight but collapses backwards.

– So how come you got into this state, Nechuparello, you pig's rectum?

The time has come for Rilke. I've got to take it out and read for ten minutes, pretend that I want to write something down and get the notebook out.

– What's her surname?

– Korshakljubory.

– What sort of Ljubory, vagina mouth?

– Korshak Ljubov Borysivna.

No better not write anything down. The junior lieutenant is watching. He's clever. Not used to anyone writing in here. If he snatches the notebook, then that could be it.

– How come she's got a different surname?

Nechuparello begins to give an amazingly eloquent and ornate account of what had happened in the war, of a woman who wasn't quite faithful, of a man who came back home without an arm, of himself at that time just a snotty kid, and of somebody else, who grabbed an axe and shouted – Stop you bastard! Can't you see he's just a baby?

Nechuparello burst into tears.

– And you – he leaps at the junior lieutenant – you have no right to badmouth my mother!

The policemen close in – Shut up, you brainless vodka bottle! – Who do you think you are, eh? – Come on, turn out your pockets, loosen your belt, get those clothes off, you discharge from the penis of a walrus!

But what if all this blows over? If the expert doesn't come and want to see it, then I'll have ruined the notebook.

– Sit down, Mykolo. Make a list of everything that's in his pockets. You, you turn them out, come on.

I start to slip open the cord of my rucksack. The junior lieutenant fixes me with his stare, the book of poetry and the notebook are at the bottom, this vortex is sucking me, down down, Jesus Christ have mercy on me! I take out an apple from the top. All the thick necks turn towards me. I pretend that the apple is sour, express this with my face, hands, shoulders, trainers, socks that it's sour, yeah a real crab apple, phooey, it's shrivelling! I stick it back inside, have mercy on me Christ, into the rucksack, tighten the cord, smile at them, oh, what a funny little fellow Nechuparello is!

– Turn everything out, I said. And you, what do you think you're gawking at? – I shrug sorry, nothing.

– Of course, sir – Nechuparello doesn't mind.

The sergeant is listing everything.

– OK, money? Vovka, count how much he's got.

– Small change …one ruble twelve .. ok .. thirty … hey, what's this?

– That's half a crown, pure silver, nineteen twenty six.

– Where did you nick this from, hedgehog?

– It's mine.

– I'm asking where you got it from.

– I always had it.

– How do you mean, 'always had it'? Did you mint it yourself, eh? – Policeman Vovka puts it between his teeth to check it out. – Three rubles ten .. four rubles .. four rubles ninety .. and what's this? – The sergeant is examining a foreign coin.

– Who did you screw this off?

– It's a present.

The policemen circle round.

– What country is it from?

– Any stupid male member knows that ... Poland.

– Can't be Poland – the junior lieutenant says.

Each policeman tries to solve the puzzle. Different countries are suggested. America, Afghanistan, and quite unexpectedly, Guadalupe.

– Hey you! – They call over to me.

Jesus Christ have mercy on me!

– What education have you got?

– Higher, though incomplete – Jesus Christ get me out of here and throw me back on the road, a helpless filing, away from this odious hole.

– What country is this from?

I pick up the coin.

– Spain.

– You see, you defecator, Guadelupan whore, you pinched it from someone and forgot about it.

– No I didn't pinch it from nobody – the defecator gets uptight – Look, I was on my way to Zahloby, felt tired, dozed off for a bit. But this coin was presented to me by my nephew.

– Nephew – echoes the junior lieutenant, then adds a new word made by prefixing the word for the male sexual organ to the final syllable of 'nephew'. The policemen guffaw in unison. Out of Nechuparello's pocket some copper coins fall on the bench, then down to the ground, followed by a shiny ring: Vovka checks it with his teeth – Aluminium!; a rubber stamp which prints *Paid: Young Communist League* (Nechuparello can't explain what he needs this for); a tiny screw; tobacco dross and something wrapped up in newspaper.

While the search is on, I dive into my rucksack, grope around for the books, fake a huge yawn and swim up to the surface with my find.

– What the hell's this? Unwrap it.

Police like treasure hunters crowd together round the small paper parcel.

– That's a gift from Indira Gandhi.

With yellow fingers like overripe cucumbers, Vovka carefully so as not to break anything extracts from the crumpled folds an Indian condom.

The telephone rings.

I take out the book, put the notebook under it, and while the police express their doubts as to whether a useless wretch like Leonyd Mikitovych is capable of using that thing, I search for the beginning of the summary of Nicholas Berdyayev's *Dostoyevsky's Disposition*.

The lieutenant replaces the receiver and says hurriedly that an external inspector is on the way. Nechuparello without belt or shoe lace, with pockets inside out, is stuffed into a cell. Somebody grabs a broom and starts sweeping the floor, another drags the bench closer to the wall.

– Hey kid! You there! Untie that rope – the lieutenant gestures to the door which is secured to the bench by a thick cord.

Having found the right page I insert Rilke as a marker and ask:

– What if I just cut it?

– Ok just cut it.

With one blow from the policeman's knife, I sever the ratline and while the melee is swarming around me (Jesus Christ have mercy on me!) I turn my back to the room praying that no one will spot what I'm doing (Ok what's up) I just want to go to the toilet (I had sexual intercourse with all your mothers) floozies, whores, dogs of female sex (Jesus Christ!) and rip out the sheet on which is written with my own hand the idealist-philosopher's name.

A car pulls up at the door. The junior lieutenant rushes out, and gallantly plunges into the dust cloud. I compress in my hand a burning sheet of paper while inside me an express train bolts across the abyss at full speed. The rails are shuddering, the engine driver casts a frightened glance into the jaws of the tunnel and covers his eyes ...

The police inspector seems to change his mind. Instead of coming in, he asks something through the car window and moves off.

The junior lieutenant comes in looking relieved and gives me a wink.

– Well who's wearing the brown trousers then?

He turns to ask a colleague:

– Whose jeep is that over there? The number isn't local. And here am I with two punctures and four bald tyres. And what kind of male sexual organ is that sitting at the wheel? See to it, Vovka.

– May I go to the toilet? I ask.

He turns to the sergeant – Tolya, show the guy where to go.

– Oh sure – says Tolya, who is at least twenty years older than him – I'll just run and do it. – But he doesn't move, he just leans back in his seat and picks his nose, all the time looking at the lieutenant like he's saying get somebody else for your gofor.

– Uh huh, uh huh – the junior lieutenant grunts through clenched teeth but Tolya doesn't bother. The lieutenant turns and beckons to me, then leads me outside to a wooden piss house in the corner of the back yard. I go in, he waits outside.

I stand above the hole, release a waterfall of urine, crumple that piece of paper, cross myself – Come on! – and watch Berdyayev and Dostoyevsky disappear into oblivion.

Jesus Christ thank you very much!

After an hour the senior lieutenant summoned me upstairs, told me to sign my story about the 'Mensheviks in Georgia' papers, gave me my passport and let me go.

For several kilometres I was floating down the road, loosening my stiffness, relaxing the tension. The haystacks were smiling invitingly, but I knew all too well now why we don't do it in the road.

A lorry with a tarpaulin cover picked me up and took me straight towards the south. I was wondering what other surprises this road would conjure up for me. But being unable to divine the future, I just dipped my eyes into the space ahead and watched it fly inside of me, to rest there for all time.

(Translation by the author/R. A. Jamieson)

Frans Masereel's illustrations to Hugh MacDiarmid

In the late 1960s Frans Masereel accepted a commission to illustrate Hugh MacDiarmid's *A Drunk Man Looks at the Thistle*. The woodcuts which resulted linked two of the great European internationalists of the twentieth-century and became part of the outstanding edition of the poem printed by Giovanni Mardersteig and published by Kulgin Duval and Colin Hamilton in 1969. *Edinburgh Review* would like to thank Michael Grieve and the publishers for permission to reproduce here all eight woodcuts and accompanying passages of the poem.

I AMNA FOU' sae muckle as tired – deid dune.
It's gey and hard wark coupin' gless for gless
Wi' Cruivie and Gilsanquhar and the like,
And I'm no' juist as bauld as aince I wes.

The elbuck fankles in the coorse o' time,
The sheckle's no' sae souple, and the thrapple
Grows deef and dour: nae langer up and doun
Gleg as a squirrel speils the Adam's apple.

Forbye, the stuffie's no' the real Mackay.
The sun's sel' aince, as sune as ye began it,
Riz in your vera saul: but what keeks in
Noo is in truth the vilest 'saxpanny planet'.

I seek, in this captivity,
To pierce the veils that darklin' fa'
– See white clints slidin' to the sea,
And hear the horns o' Elfland blaw.

I ha'e dark secrets' turns and twists,
A sun is gi'en to me to haud,
The whisky in my bluid insists,
And spiers my benmaist history, lad.

And owre my brain the flitterin'
O' the dim feathers gangs aince mair,
And, faddomless, the dark blue glitterin'
O' twa een in the ocean there.

Or a muckle bellows blawin'
Wi' the sperks a' whizzin' oot;
Or green tides sweeshin'
'Neth heich-skeich stars,
Or centuries fleein' doun a water-chute.

Grinnin' gargoyle by a saint,
Mephistopheles in Heaven,
Skeleton at a tea-meetin',
Missin' link – or creakin'
Hinge atween the deid and livin' ....

(I kent a Terrier in a sham fecht aince,
Wha louped a dyke and landed on a thistle.
He'd naething on ava aneth his kilt.
Schönberg has nae notation for his whistle.) ...

But I can gi'e ye kindness, lad,
And a pair o' willin' hands,
And you sall ha'e my breists like stars,
My limbs like willow wands,

Guid sakes, ye dinna need to pass
Ony exam. to dee
– Daith canna tell a common flech
Frae a performin' flea! ...

It sets you weel to slaver
To let sic gaadies fa'
– *The mune's the muckle white whale*
I seek in vain to kaa!

My Earth's my mastless samyn,
The thistle my ruined sail.
 – Le'e go as you maun in the end,
And droon in your plumm o' ale! ...

I saw a rose come loupin' oot
Frae a camsteerie plant.
O wha'd ha'e thocht yon puir stock had
Sic an inhabitant?

For centuries in ran to waste,
Wi' pin-heid floo'ers at times.
O'ts hidden hert o' beauty they
Were but the merest skimes.

Yet while it ran to wud and thorns,
The feckless growth was seekin'
Some airt to cheenge its life until
A' in a rose was beekin'.

I'm under nae delusions, fegs!
The whuppin' sooker at wha's tip
Oor little point o' view appears,
A midget coom o' continents
Wi' blebs o' oceans set, sends up
The braith o' daith as weel as life,
And we maun braird anither tip
Oot owre us ere we wither tae,
And join the sentrice skeleton
As coral insects big their reefs.

Hoo money men to mak' a man
It tak's he kens wha kens Life's plan.

But there are flegsome deeps
Whaur the soul o' Scotland sleeps
That I to bottom need
To wauk Guid kens what deid,
Play at stertle-a-stobie,
Wi' nation's dust for hobby,
Or wi' God's sel' commerce
For the makin' o' a verse.

ENCYCLOPAEDIA SUPPLEMENT

Politics improving our native land,
We lectured and preached by women and men.
But we gotta know, friends, what you talking about
As you're sure to pay darn dear for your mouth.
So, if you know you can't use the knife and fork,
They mean to license we mouth, they don't want we talk.

King Radio

As you approach London on the train from the north, you notice that it appears to have spilled over its proper boundaries. Optimists, and those with a vested interest, would say that this indicates a flourishing nation; but the truth of the matter is that it is not so much a case of 'His cup runneth over' as the feeling one has on entering a mens' urinal (beckoned by Nature) to discover the tiled floor so deep in water &c as to form a kind of tide as the door swings open. Many a pair of training shoes has been ruined that way, many a tear shed over plimsolls that had four or five years more wear in them. Thus confronted, a silent retreat seems to be the only option. To piss on the floor, as many have evidently done before you, would simply be uncivilised.

The *Encyclopaedia* is intended as a mop. You – reader, no sexual exclusivity is intended in the use of the above metaphor – are urged to make use of it. It is anticipated that the overflow will not cease: indeed, its swirls and eddies are likely to become imprinted on the mind's eye until they are as familiar and as vertiginous as those in the shower scene from Hitchcock's 'Psycho'. But the effort must be made, or may as well be made.

Phil Ochs wrote: 'In such an ugly time, the true protest is beauty'. You do not need to be Keats or Schiller to produce something beautiful; and to recognise ugliness, you need only be alive and currently residing in the UK. Contributions to the *Encyclopaedia* – provocations, polemic, memoirs, *textes trouvées*, notes – should be short, legible and literate. Particularly welcome, as the *Edinburgh Review* begins to appear on a more regular basis, are novel explanations of misunderstood contemporary trends and phenomena. Bias will be shown towards those pieces which seem lucid, pertinent, grammatically sound and enlightening. So as not to disappoint contributors, let it be known that the current editorial line for this section is frankly – in some cases, redemptively – interventionist and proceeds empirically, with one eye on the overall shape of each issue and the other eye on the clock.

A CONSPIRACY OF GOOD TASTE

In 1971 the Scratch Orchestra visited Newcastle and the north east to do its 'dealer concert' series. These became notorious through the media sensationalising Greg Bright's piece 'Sweet FA'. It was reported that in this piece Cornelius Cardew wrote 'fuck' on pieces of paper and handed them to children.

At about this time I was preparing my study of basic shelters, later to be published by Unicorn Books in Brighton as 'Survival Scrapbook 1: Shelter'. Unicorn books had recently been taken to court, I think for selling 'The Little Red Schoolbook'. We were camping just outside Newcastle near the village of Overton. Across a little river was a brightly painted group of about fifty 'shanty' houses. These intrigued me with their inventive adaptations of sheds and vans. The improvised collage of found materials had a parallel to our activity in the Orchestra and I took a morning off to capture these images on a roll of slide film. Later, as I travelled about, I discovered more and more of these settlements all over the country. Although I wrote articles about them for 'Architectural Design' and 'Radical Technology', it was to be almost another twenty years before the full implication of my fascination with these structures became clear to me.

This realisation was facilitated recently, first through an unpublished thesis by Phil Wren at Hull School of Architecture. In this he pointed out that the growth of British shanties was a result of the availability to the proletariat of increased leisure time. He quoted Clough Williams Ellis (influential in the Amenity and New town movements and the designer of Portmerion) who pronounced that shanties were 'England's most disfiguring disease'.

Then I walked in on a TV programme that was showing how the revered Arts & Crafts movement of Ruskin and Morris had created a romantic myth about the British countryside which had fed the formation of modern nationalism in the build up to the First World War. Unfortunately I didn't find out the name of the programme or its director. The implications of what I had seen only sank in slowly.

Some time later, in a dustbin, I found a couple of copies of Folk Music Journal, one of which contained a review of Pete Harker's Fakesong: The manufacture of British folksong from 1700 to the present day. This argues that Cecil Sharpe, who was a major figure in defining British Folk Music, misrepresented working class culture.

By now my suspicions were well developed.

As the cities grew with industrialisation the potential for a new working class culture became apparent. This would have posed a great threat to capitalism. Before any such stage could be reached, however, it was cleverly diverted, distorted and misrepresented by various middle class philanthropists and socialists to the point at which the working class were finally denied 'culture' at all!

It is hard for us to comprehend or feel the enormity and violence of oppression on this scale. The results of it have become so much a part of our mundane reality. Certainly it left me amazed. At the same time it went a long way to explain how I felt about the Art and Culture around me.

Howard Slater and I determined to study all this a bit more thoroughly. We quickly became aware that historians liked Stephen and Eileen Yeo had been onto this for a few years and, again rather by chance, came across a new book by Chris Waters British Socialists and the politics of Popular culture, 1884-1914. This suggested to me that socialism was never truly a working class liberation movement, but had been taken over by a series of 'well heeled' middle class leaders who interpreted the 'elevation' of the working classes entirely in terms of their own values. This process was facilitated by the mechanics of oppression which meant that many working class leaders believed the negative stereotypes of working class people held out by the ruling class and saw their betterment only in middle class terms.

The philanthropists of the 19th century had tried to engage the working classes in their newly won leisure time with 'Rational Recreation': choral singing, walks in the country, going to art galleries, reading books and that sort of thing. Orderly unemotional pastimes. The masses, however, needed self-generated activities with more emotional involvement and expression, like football and music hall. These sorts of activities were increasingly provided and controlled by commercial interests.

To be denied a culture is to be denied the possibility of developing social and economic relations that benefit all people. No liberation movement can be successful without autonomous cultural assertion. It is here that the reformation and reforging of values, which allow new social relations to evolve, occurs.

I think that we now need to fight to establish a redefinition and development of working class culture on our own terms. The massive influx of the lower classes into tertiary education in the past few decades has put us into many positions of cultural power unprecedented in history. We are now strong enough to contact each other and together assert our class identity and interest.

If you wish to get a copy of a research and discussion bulletin on topics raised above, to be edited by Howard Slater, please contact.

STEFAN SZCZELKUN.
85 St Agnes Place,
London SE11 4BB

Further Reading

Class Myths & Culture, Stefan Szczelkun, Working Press 1990.

DIASPORIST MANIFESTO

R. B. Kitaj's *First Diasporist Manifesto* was published in 1989 by Thames & Hudson. An assimilated Jewish American painter, long resident in London, his purpose is to explain and justify the power of idiosyncracy and a critically distanced perspective in life and in art. And he assures us that we don't have to be Jewish to be a Diasporist.

The term 'Diaspora' has come to refer to the position of Jews outside the Holy Land, dispersed with the destruction of the Temple in 70 AD. They became 'rootless cosmopolitans', to use the ultimate

insult from Stalin's later anti-semitic rages. Some would always have believed that an element of rootless cosmopolitanism is a critical part of the concept 'modern' and indeed a critical element in the idea of education.

Within high culture, the work of Diasporists in all disciplines must form an honourable conundrum. As Kitaj notes, within art in his time, half the painters of the great schools of Paris, New York and London were not born in their host countries. But there is also the role of internal exile, with a depressive connection providing its own aesthetic. He lists here not only Primo Levi and Franz Kafka, but Haim Soutine and Mark Rothko. While Vladimir Nabokov was able to combine his inner grieving for Russia with the exhilaration of new experiences of languages and cultures in the sardonic *Pnin* and the fabulous *Lolita*, Walter Benjamin becomes the ultimate tragic Diasporist, who rationally saw suicide as the only solution.

Exile may be physical or experiential. Its discontents appear as subtly and unclearly in the work of refugees as they do in the inner exile of women and gays. Black intellectuals too are increasingly defining their position as Diasporist (see Maud Sulter's poem *Zabat*, Urban Fox Press). Scots express a high diasporist energy, although not necessarily linking themselves with other outsiders.

Unsurprisingly, Kitaj, himself embodies diasporism and, in Diasporist Painting (which school he caused to exist by his book), displays its idiosyncratic quality – fractured, because the narrative content itself is enacted metaphorically in two or more societies. Consequent to his cognitive position, his genre of parable paintings is criticised for being 'littered with ideas' – an insult he bears proudly. He says he has been a good bad boy. After all, not since 1912 have artists been able to succumb to the simple pleasures of paint. There is more to a painting than what can be seen in it: 'The Idea is the silver lining in art.' This is what distinguishes a critical figurative painting from the narrative of the Academy.

If psychologists since Freud acknowledge that there is a human impulse to resolve ambiguity, Kitaj believes that the task of modern thinking is also to understand that indeterminacy of meaning is compatible with truth. Then, as Kitaj suggests, Diasporism may be a form of self-definition that proudly pursues a homelesss logic of *ethnie*.

HALLA BELOFF

'DULCE ET DECORUM EST ...'

In relation to Wilfred Owen's *Dulce et Decorum Est'*, a strong irony results from what we know of the author of the maxim *'Dulce et decorum est pro patria mori'* Horace was not the actual originator of the phrase. It is extremely likely that Horace would have been familiar with Homer's line, 'It is not unseemly for a man to die fighting in defence of his country' (*Iliad*, XV, 1. 496). Horace was steeped in ancient Greek poetry and he so believed in the superiority of Greek poetry over Roman poetry that he refers to the history of Latin literature only as a coda to the story of the time when 'Greece took her captor captive' (*'Graecia capta ferum uictorem cepti'*). Horace established his reputation by writing Latin poetry distinctly indebted to Greek poets, notably following Archilochus (probably 8th century BC) and Alcaeus (born about 620 BC). Although Owen quoted Horace ironically, there is no reason to believe that Homer was paraphrased ironically by Horace (in the sentence quoted by Owen from one of the Roman Odes) [*Odes,* III, ii, 13]. Indeed Horace was an unofficial poet laureate in the time of Augustus Caesar, with the attendant necessity that Horace uphold in these odes the virtues of the Augustan age, such as 'moderation (No. 1), frugality combined with valour (No. 2), justice and *grauitas* (No. 3), patriotism (No. 5), piety (No. 6)' [H J Rose, *A Handbook of Latin Literature,* 3rd ed., London, 1954, page 274].

One question that arises from Horace's other writings is whether Horace really was the man best suited to write the bravely patriotic sentiments inferred from his words, *'Dulce et decorum est pro patria mori'*. Quintus Horatius Flaccus

was a military tribune (a staff officer attached to a legion) in the army of Brutus and was caught up in the fighting at Philippi (42 BC). When the civil war was over, Horace returned to Rome only to discover that his father had died and that his farm had been given to demobilized soldiers who had fought on the winning side instead of that which Horace had volunteered to support. He therefore had to buy himself a job as a *scriba quaestorius* (a clerk in the finance department of the civil service) and says he took up the writing of poetry to supplement his meagre income.

An irony echoing over the millenia, due to Owen's quotation from Horace, comes from an admission Horace made about his performance at Philippi. In a verse epistle to his friend Pompeius, who was involved in the same military encounter, he wrote, 'We two once beat a swift retreat together / Upon Philippi's field, / When I dumped my poor shield, / And courage cracked'. Horace was 'half-dead with fear'. (Ode 7, *The Odes of Horace,* trans. by James Michie, Harmondsworth, 1964, pages 102-103) Many critics have tried to explain away Horace's confession of his cowardice. This is in spite of the fact that over the score of centuries intervening between this admission, all critics who have praised him have singled out one of his most attractive qualities in words strikingly similar to Sir Paul Harvey's phrase, the 'sincerity and frankness of his self-portraiture'. Both Alcaeus and Archilochus also admit to abandoning their shields in battle; so, goes the argument, Horace was probably only following a poetic tradition when he wrote of his cowardice. Horace may have been trying to undercut the significance of the fact that he had been in the army opposed to Augustus. But his confession should be examined in contrast to the wording of his poetic sources before readers leap to the conclusion made by those who dismiss his words as mere poetic pretence.

Archilochus's actual words were, 'Some Thracian now enjoys my shield, which I left unwillingly on a bush, though it was quite undamaged. But I saved myself. Why should I worry about that shield – let it go! I will get another which will be just as good'. Here is the abandoned shield - but where is the cowardice? Horace's words clearly imply that he willingly left his shield at Philippi; Archilochus insists that he abandoned his shield unwillingly. Furthermore, Archilochus looks forward to being in battle again: 'I will get another which will be just as good'. This is not the stuff of cowardice. Notably no friend is involved in the incident of Archilochus's lost shield and his 'saving' of himself. The words of Alcaeus come to us in a very corrupt fragment, so their interpretation is uncertain; but they must mean something like, 'Alcaeus is safe, but the Athenians hung up (?his armour, ?his protective shield) in the temple of grey-eyed Athena'. Again, there is no explicit mention of cowardice or running here. These are simple statements: he is safe, the enemy has his shield as a trophy.

Therefore there is no evidence that there was a poetic tradition specifically mentioning *cowardice* and *running away* from battle. The Greek poetic tradition did not mention running away because to have done so would have been redundant repetition; a man who lost his shield had to run away or be killed; the fact that one survived to write about the loss meant that the mention of a lost shield was symbolic shorthand for retreat. It is noteworthy that although Alcaeus wrote about the loss of his shield to his friend, the poet did not implicate his friend in the ignominy of the situation. In passing we should mention that Anacreon, a poet writing in the second half of the sixth century BC, is quoted as 'having thrown away a shield by the banks of a fair-flowing river', but this fragment of words (cited with no context, to illustrate a metrical point by a late Roman grammatical writer) is all we have of this item. Again there is no explicit mention of funk or running away.

The biggest difficulty with the arguments put forward to prove that Horace did not really mean that he ran from battle to protect his own hide, is that they go against the grain of Horace's otherwise honest self-portraiture, his 'sincerity' and his 'frankness'. To say that Horace was scheming enough to adopt the device of employing ancient Greek sources by way of crawling to Augustus is perhaps more damning even than granting that he may have been telling the mere truth about his disgraceful performance at Philippi and that he found a convenient literary tradition to hand when it came to expressing his shame.

If Horace's claims are supposed to be in the tradition of Archilochus and Alcaeus, his departures from the 'tradition' are such important twists as to set his confession apart from the 'tradition'. Unlike Archilochus and Alcaeus, Horace not only claims that he abandoned his shield, but he goes against the 'tradition' by explicitly spelling out that he *ran away* from battle. He also breaks with the 'tradition' in another way, in that Archilochus and Alcaeus both mention only their *personal* involvement in the incidents cited, whereas Horace goes out of his way to mention that his friend Pompeius and he 'beat a hasty retreat together'.

Edward Fraenkel, citing previous critics, asks why Horace insisted 'on such a drastic sign of cowardice?' The answer is to be sought in two directions. First, 'the mode in which he makes his confession is in accordance with his habitual candour and ironical self-depreciation' Secondly, the friend to whom the ode *O saepe mecum* is addressed survived because he took part in the *celeris fuga* from Philippi. That was an undeniable fact. But the last thing Horace would wish to do was to hurt his friend's feelings. He therefore speaks of his own soldierly deficiency in the crudest possible manner. 'It is characteristic of Horace that he will always ascribe also to himself any particular weakness with which a friend has to be charged ... Instances of this tactful expression of his fellow-feeling are to be found throughout Horace's work; in the *Epistles* they are of special importance'. However, although this assertion of pretence springing from a selfless motive is tempting, it necessarily undercuts the words Fraenkel quoted from W Y Sellar about Horace's 'habitual candour'. All in all, it is perhaps best to take Horace at his word about his funk in this one crucial instance.

Wilfred Owen, whose acquaintance with Latin was skimpy and whose knowledge of Horace's life and poetry was probably slim at best, is unlikely to have know just how ironic his use of the quotation from Horace actually was.

PHILLIP WHIDDEN

EUROPEAN THEATRICAL DANCE

The story of European Theatrical dance can be broached by pointing to one very specific development: the gradual shortening of the female Ballet dancer's dress from ankle-length to waist-height, revealing as fully as possible the legs and groin area of the dancer. This development took approximately 150 years (circa 1700-1850). The 'inherent' disreputable 'nature' of a woman revealing as much of her primary and secondary sexual characteristics as she could (without actually going bottomless) was recognised in the nineteenth and early twentieth centuries – an age in which the sight of a pretty woman's ankle in public sparked off libidinous explosions of male fantasies; an age in which the most important art critic of the century was shocked to discover, after marrying, that women had pubic hair.

So-called Classical Ballet (it is actually *Romantic* Ballet) was in many senses, popular art, and thus considered vulgar. Generally, Ballet dancers were part of the illegitimate theatre and were regarded as unofficial courtesans by wealthy men. Some time between 1900 and 1950, ballet dancers acquired the status of artists (as opposed to *artistes*), the storm-troupers of this battle for respectability being dancers like Pavlova, de Valois (founder of English Royal Ballet), and Rambert (founder of Ballet Rambert). This layer of artistic respectability, masking what is a quite obvious commercial display of sexually active visual images, has enormously confused the historiography of dance and our present understanding of what dance is.

To put it crudely, nineteenth century Romantic Ballet was a circus style entertainment, wherein professional entertainers gave an extremely garbled and distorted imitation of seventeenth century courtly social dance, as part of a show where shapely limbs were put through difficult movements designed to show off both their physical beauty and acrobatic virtuosity. Overlaying this was a set of sentimental narratives, normally about Romantic/doomed love.

A resemblance (rather superficial) between the dance poses and those of ancient Greek and Renaissance sculpture served as a further spurious cloak of respectability behind which male patrons could, among other things, satisfy proto-pornographic tendencies.

Because of the enormous (if problematic) veneer of respectability that now surrounds Ballet (Margot Fonteyn is an icon for the middling classes almost as potent as the Queen Mother herself), it is almost impossible to see the historical origins of ballet. These *origins* do *not* go back primarily to European social dancing in the courts of Medieval and Renaissance Europe. Rather they are much more rooted in a variety of commercial and semi-commercial entertainments perhaps most effectively, if crudely, denoted by the terms 'circus' and pantomime'.

The plausibility of this account has been demonstrated by Belinda Quirey with extremely detailed reconstructions of the relationship between dance techniques and the accompanying music. This history of technique closely parallels the development of 'dance' as a theatrical activity in the growing commercial entertainment industry of the eighteenth and nineteenth centuries. The main point here is that the pre-Romantic, pre-Theatrical dance of European courts was an extremely subtle response to the intricate rhythms of the music, done by all of those present (collectively or individually) for the felt pleasure of the movement as an extension of the music. Those who watched enjoyed watching because they also had done similar movements at similar levels of skilled musicality. In terms of jargon the pleasure of dancing was largely proprioceptive and social, and when watched, the viewer had a kinaesthetic empathy with the proprioceptive and social pleasure of the dancer. (This is not to deny the obvious 'spectacular' functions of European social dance.)

Dance was not seen: it was felt. Dance in the courts, as in the peasant villages, had been a participant activity. It aspired, to garble Pater, to the condition of the human voice in conversation or in song – several could 'talk' at once, each performer being simultaneously an audience, and each participant helping to push a set of *actions*, in a collective whole, through time.

Ballet (Theatrical Ballet that is) was very much to be seen. Poses were often struck, and the technique of ballet consisted in learning how to perform difficult movements holding the body in rigid positions that imitated (emulated) painted or sculpted images. The experience of the dancer was irrelevant – especially the proprioceptive pleasures of responding to the music. Ballet aspires to the condition of a monumental image – observed, studied for its iconic and emotive meanings, and so on.

If Ballet were nothing but an entertainment, it would not be a terrible thing. But Ballet has become a Platonic ideal of which all other forms of dancing are but pale reflections. Even when the overt forms of ballet are denied (the pointed foot, the rigid pelvis, etc), the underlying theatrical principles are not. (This applies to Graham, Nikolai, Cunningham and most New Dance.)

The interaction between spectacular performance and mutual participatory forms of cultural activity are always complex but never more opposed than they are in modern culture, and this opposition never more clearly and importantly demonstrated than in dance. The notion that most of us need *not* learn to dance or sing because these are essentially *spectacular entertainments* and *specialised art forms*, emerges most clearly since the mid-eighteenth century in Europe, with the rise of ballet, opera, and symphonic music.

It is something like a society saying it doesn't need most of its members to learn how to have conversations, to make jokes,

etc, because enjoyment of these will be vicariously provided by TV shows. The confusion is deep: the existential (ontological) status of dance performed on a stage (or TV studio) as an entertainment is qualitatively different from that of dance danced collectively by participants.

Theatrical dance is effectively an imitation, an illusion, of the 'real' dance of social participation. Speech has a similar situation in the theatre: the 'speech' of actors on a stage is ontologically different from speech practised by people off-stage. Linguistic theory (Austin, Searle, Derrida) as far as I know doesn't deal with this ontological division between Western 'theatrical' communication and other modes. (This division is, I believe, *ontological*, rather than epistemological, and therefore can't be reduced to analytical categories used to describe *all* communication e.g. locutionary/illocutionary; enoncé/enonciation. That is, the distinction between 'theatrical' and 'real' communication does *not* denote two aspects of the same phenomenon.)

Surely it's partly indicative of modernity that we find nothing strange in going to watch people imitate a dance (on stage) which basically no longer exists in reality? Even worse, we confuse the imitation for the 'real thing'? When actors speak lines, we *know*, still, that these actors do not mean what they say – that the actors and the playwright have collaborated to produce an *imitation* of what real persons might say to each other – a real conversation is not taking place on the stage. To put it into jargon, the conditions of enunciation determine the ontological status of the action; or more intelligibly, the relations between 'performers' and between 'performers' and those 'observing' determine the meaning of the action.

Ballet and its derivative, theatrical dance (like theatrical 'speech') therefore is not real dance. It is an *imitation* of dance, as theatrical speech is an *imitation* of real speech. No one ever takes a conversation on a stage or screen for real conversation between real people – so why do we confuse dance on stage or screen with real dance done by real people? The simple answer is: because real dance no longer exists. The complicated answer needs a little more discussion-time. (N.B. The same confusion obscures discussions of music.)

MO DODSON

Further Reading:
The 'standard' history: *The Dancer's Heritage* by Ivor Ernest c. 1968 and *Ballet & Modern Dance* by Susan Au c. 1988. The critique of this standard history is only partly articulated in Belinda Quirey's *May I have the Pleasure* 1976, and in her earlier articles in the *Dancing Times* Oct. 1969 to Jan. 1971 'Apology for History' in 8 parts (co-authored with Michael Holmes). The full extent and implications of her work remain unpublished. There are very few histories of theatrical dance as such, but there is an extremely exhaustive account by Richard Ralph of the career of John Weaver, a dancing-master who established commercial theatrical dance and pantomime in London in the first half of the Eighteenth Century.

THE EXCITING WORLD OF CHEESE
The publication of *City Limits* 'Streetwise Cheese Guide' affords a fine opportunity for a snapshot view at the way in which Britain's cutting edge left-wing intellectuals are coming to terms with problem of cheese selection in the uncertain climate of the nineties. Camembert is definitely out – as Helen Strzelecki points out in one of her most characteristic pieces of gourmet criticism. Strzelecki's argument is a stinging judgement on the whole myth-structure of the French soft cheese (Roquefort being an honorable exception). The lactic texture, alluding as it must surely do to certain pubescent male constructs of feminity, informs the cheese's penetration of the nasal cavity – reversing this vexatious concept of female passivity into a symbolic code for gender violation. And simply to 'cut a slice' of these cheeses involves the slashing or hacking of a thick, creamy white skin, *prized* for its whiteness. In the end, we're relieved to move on to less harrowing fare.

Dan Draper offers a deconstructionalist reading of the French full-cream mountain cheeses, with a full-length case study of a Reblochon which he served at a recent on-campus party at USC, as part of his PHD dissertation cheese-and-wine party. Draper's problem is an essential one – in the absence of accepted social norms, how is one to 'read' the flavour of such a cheese? Clearly the formalist notions of meaning in relation to supposed 'contrasts' with other, comparable foodstuffs (some of these not even cheeses at all!) would hardly stand up even to pre-Post Structuralist analysis, or to the kind of neo-Marxist Tel Quel enthusiasm peddled by Sam Shepperton in his *Local History of Cheddar Cheeses* (Macmillan, 1983). Draper is concerned with the formal creation of a critical language of the taste buds, a technique which will allow a more meaningful 'eating' to take place. He stresses the political divisions inherent in the distinction drawn between 'eating' and 'tasting', and develops this bipolarity into a deconstruction of the discourses involved in non-eating (~~eating~~) and non-tasting (~~tasting~~). The pleasure of the text is chiefly a series of *anticipations* – the gratifying ability to 'read' (~~taste~~) the cheese fully in accordance with the structural language of our expectations. But when does (~~tasting~~) deconstruct into (~~eating~~) – the ultimate non-consumption of the wine taster (or ~~drinker~~) who spits out his drink when its elusive flavour has been labelled? (~~Eating~~) ultimately becomes (~~living~~), as one is no longer able to read even the discourse of a rumbling tummy, and begins to miss meals without knowing it – entering the state of starvation (~~food~~) – a complete inability to arrive at a coherent reading of the 'text' – from a sausage roll to a seven course banquet.

What, then, of the highly structured (~~eatings~~) which are fostered by the hermetically sealed environment of advertising? Renate Agostini-Clark offers a fascinating reading of television cheese commercials, where the white, malleable, flocculent, substance of the product is presented as a sacramental mediating substance, not unlike the honey offered in Samoan Cultures in ritual expression of the passage into womanhood and the onset of menstruation. But what about mozzarella? Agostini-Clark is in no doubt. This seminal, milky substance stands for the eternally adolescent vexations of Italian and Latin society, locked into its own internal male rigidity – 'lacking even the yellow evolutionary moulding into our experience of a protestant cheese such as cheddar or Monterey Jack.' And what about the cheeses of tomorrow? Agostini-Clark is in no doubt that they will reflect the increasingly hidebound but invisible compartmentalization of late capitalist society. 'Soft, but unyielding, unlocalized, seductively strong-flavoured, even a little sweet, fragrant, pleasant to chew – but no after-flavour, and no sharp surge of pleasure on the taste buds.' A terrifying vision, maybe, of life in the twenty-first century?

CLUBBER KLUBER

GRANVILLE & HEILGERS

I think I must be an unacknowledged masochist, or possibly just willing myself to fail, but I'm forever being toyed, experimented and tantalised by literary obscurity. Consciously, though, I can map the associative track that took me to that strange, dual mystery, Charles Granville (1867–?) and Louise Heilgers (1880–?), two specks of froth on the literary waters of this century's first decades.

I reached Granville via the *New Age*. Not that he was ever much of a contributor thereto; a stray poem, an occasional letter, little more. But, in 1912, Beatrice Hastings, *New Age*'s all-purpose staff-writer, she of the lashing, trashing answer, the return salvo in the sex war, eminently-pursuable, voluptuous Beatrice, wrote an allegorical novel, by instalments, for the magazine. It is an anonymous work, titled the 'Maids' Comedy', a bizarre, indigestible, conversational tale of a feminist donna Quixote and Sancho Panza, riding over the Transvaal veldt, encountering mounted, male chauvinism, and subduing it.

They (Orage, 'N.A.'s' editor, and Co) had to find a publisher, and persuaded the firm of Stephen Swift to take it. There was no Stephen, nor indeed any Swift; the front concealed the identity of Charles

Granville. And this name was a dissimulation also, a fact which might never have been revealed without the precise reporting of Granville's trial for bigamy and embezzlement twelve months later in *The Times*. There he was unmasked as Charles Hosken, formerly of Helston, Cornwall, by profession a solicitor's clerk, a not inconsiderable poet (one of his poems was in the Oxford Book of Victorian Verse), a double bigamist, and a reliever of a naive academic investor of a sum of, roughly, a thousand pounds.

Even despite the relentlessly respectable standards of The Times, Granville's trial must have been a literary *cause celebre*. Orage, never a man to undersell his friends in need, described the defendant as an English Tolstoy, and was choked off by the Recorder for distorting the truth. Granville was sent down for twelve months penal servitude.

Here we'll recapitulate a trifle. Of one thing we can be certain, Charles Granville had a nose for talent. As extension of the Stephen Swift empire, he'd launched the liberationist *Freewoman* magazine. Dora Marsden, a true termagant, was his editor, but the contributors included Rebecca West who wrote with disemboweling intelligence and ferocity. He'd also published Ezra Pound, spiriting him away from Elkin Mathews & Co. with an overwhelming advance, having previously chastised the poet for his translation of Heine. By some mysterious alchemy, Granville had become a master of languages, describing himself thus on his first bigamous marriage certificate. Richard Orage passed him Katherine Mansfield, who was to be with him until Middleton Murry persuaded her elsewhere. And he trapped (appropriate word, as we shall see) Arthur Ransome, then in his *belles-lettres* phase.

Ransome, and his biographer, are useful sources on Granville. It's scavenging as distinct from mining, you understand, but none the less welcome in a dearth of facts. Granville had a weakness for coincidence, not quite of Koestlerian dimensions, but severe enough. I'm more than infected, myself, so conceive my astonishment when I, Bedford born and bred, learned of his caper of introducing Arthur Ransome (*Swallows and Amazons*) to Arthur Ransom (eighty year-old editor of The Bedfordshire Times and Standard). In Bedfordshire, men and women die between the shafts!

It is possible that Granville's acquaintance with Ransom grew out of a printing contract placed with the Beds. Times Press. But Granville strengthened the friendship by publishing one (perhaps two) of the old man's novels. By a strange twist of pathos, Ransom did not long survive this eventide success, dying within months. His is probably the largest interval ever recorded between first and second books. A near half-century elapsed between the publication of his little tract in the early eighteen sixties and his Stephen Swift novel in 1912.

The meeting between the two Ransomes, separated also by half a century in age and six counties in origin, was all the success hoped for by Granville. The young writer was full·of freshness and zeal; the aged editor, encouraging and gracious. They discovered common roots.

Not long after, Granville left Bedford (his sojourn had probably been a creditor-evasion tactic) and then events began to tramp along to crisis and disaster. It seems he went to a party at the Maddox Ford's. The magistrate who had given him bail on a charge of bigamy seven years before, and not clapped eyes on him since, was also a guest. What followed seems to epitomise a great loss of tolerance and fair-play, a breaking of charity, a vast gap between then and now, for the magistrate, taking Granville aside, simply warned him that he would be telephoning the police in the morning.

In the morning, Granville was on a quick boat to Tangier, possibly accompanied by his secretary. Later in the week, a desperate Arthur Ransome was camped outside the Stephen Swift offices, begging the liquidators for his manuscripts. We now know, thanks to the expert searching of John Warren in the melée of confusion which is St. Catherine's House, that Granville left somebody else behind in London, a thirty-three year old writer whose stories and novels he'd published, and who was carrying his child. Her name was Louise Heilgers. Her photograph shows a strong face, and we know her father was a wealthy East India shipper. In what was to be a life of sustained trouble, she was to need both strength and wealth.

When Charles Granville emerged from gaol (it was possibly Wandsworth), the First World War was within weeks of breaking out. This cataclysm, and Louise Heilger's baby, probably inhibited any sudden arising of a new publishing phoenix, but in 1915 a firm called Dryden & Co., out of Essex Street, appeared in the booksellers' lists.

An instructive connection can now be made across a wider writing family. The Cornish poet, James Dryden Hosken, was Charles Granville's eldest brother. Without doubt, furnishing a model for flight, he quit the family home, ten years before Charles, on a Whittingtonian foray to London. Unlike lucky Dick, he failed to find a literary lodgement. Perhaps he did not keep a cat. He did, however, keep up a piteous, forty-year, begging-letter correspondence with his one-time publisher, Macmillan.

Courteously, patiently and often generously, the partners answer him, their letters (now in the University of Reading archive) echoing deep paternalistic resonances. Not feet away in another collection, his brother Charles's more elegant appeals vibrate sympathetically.

So, Charles, like as not, borrowed his brother's middle name and, using Louise Heilger's father's money, set up a new publishing front. The lady certainly took an entrepreneurial grip on the business. One of her Flanders' anthologies came out in a tricoleur binding, looking like the wrapping from a barber's pole. Charles Granville published nothing under his pseudonym, probably because he feared his creditors might catch up with him. There is no record of his bankruptcy, however, in the Thomas More index. But there is more than a hint of ghost-writing activities and concomitant calamities in letters he wrote to Grant Richards. These hint at razor-sharp practices by a publisher, named only as Mr Jenkins, clearly an operator of a different moral calibre to the Macmillans.

Then, in 1917, Granville became acquainted with agony, and learned to know it well. Spring that year brought confused and savage fighting around Arras, and in one of the battles, Captain Basil Granville, our anti-hero's son, was killed. Useless to enquire of the Ministry of Defence the official attestation circumstances of a young twenty year old: born Hosken, but serving, commissioned, and dying, as Granville. On first enquiry, the MOD denied his military existence. Yet questions relentlessly remain. Does filial piety account for the change of name, or maybe admiration, and if the latter, by what elasticity does it encompass a failed and felon father? What is it that comes like grace to Charles Granville, and powers his finest work, the anthology, *Soldier Son*? This, practically the last book from the Dryden firm, was published in 1918, with a foreword from the Foreign Secretary, no less. Perhaps remorse and guilt are enough to jolt a talent from mediocrity to brilliance, especially if those you have matchlessly wronged, love and admire you still.

With the war almost at an end, Charles Granville moved into a post-remorse phase, marked at the onset by the birth of twin daughters to Louise Heilgers. Both girls are enormously untraceable. They did not attend school, have not married, and as far as records go, have not died. Given the hyperactivity of Louise Heilgers after their births, it's conceivable they were immediately adopted, for she seems to have gone into high gear in 1919, quitting Fulham for Richmond on Thames and establishing a creative-writing school called Correspondence College Ltd., at an exquisite Georgian house in Parkshott Terrace.

We can read Charles Granville on this change, on the College's note-paper with its list of distinguished tutors and picture of the proprietress. He shows complete reliance upon his wife's business competence, and their redemptive time to come. That this is necessity being made virtuous is not at all clear. But what *is* clear be-

yond all doubt is the trauma of Charles Granville, the impact of ten long and tortured years, upon *her*. We have two photographs of Louise on two styles of heading. The dates on the letters are separated by about a year, but the photographs contrast a *soignee* woman in her late twenties with a haggard sexagenarian of imploring gaze. There may be ten years between the two portraits, but the clothes and styles do not support this comforting notion. They were both engaged on coal-mining rather than gold-mining, and the economic depression of the 'twenties was beginning to bite.

We possess only three other secure facts about Louise Heilgers. She sold her Correspondence College Ltd. and the associated *Writer* magazine in 1926, and published a romantic novel with John Long a year later. Then there is a break of seven years. John Warren has one last trace of her in 1935, living in Clovelly, she is informant on her mother's death certificate. After that, nothing. She publishes no book, she does not remarry, die, or abjure the realm, at least according to the B.M. catalogue and those monstrous indices which range the walls of St. Catherine's House.

The University of Reading's archives hold three more Granville letters. A devotee of ancient Greek religion would proclaim them as evidence of Nemesis catching up the sins of Hubris, for they are terrible appeals for money, even the smallest sum. They are written, 1929-31, from lodgings in Honour Oak Park to a forgotten journalist called Megroz. Megroz sends a few shillings (he pens begging letters himself, most fascinatingly to St. John Adcock, the Editor of *Bookman*). Charles Granville has a plan. He will write a cameo on up-and-coming Megroz for Adcock's magazine. Nemesis has a different plan. Adcock dies, suddenly. So does his talented daughter, Marion. There is never any cameo on Megroz in *Bookman*, which shortly expires.

Last call for Charles Granville. We are left, like the jokey T. E. Lawrence, to hedge ourselves around with a few speculative hypotheses. Is our man that Charles Granville, caretaker of a block of flats in

Wimpole Street, who dies, intestate, of uraemia in 1943? Do we seek that elusive Charles Granville, who in 1941 translated a book of Czech folk-tales, in New York, for the government in exile, but who never identified himself in person to the sponsors? Did Charles Granville's mastery of languages include Czech? These are questions, for which, try and puzzle though we may, we shall probably find no answers at all.

DEAN JUNIPER

THE GREEN MOVEMENT AND PLANETARY ILLNESS: A WRONG DIAGNOSIS

If a Doctor came to you, having treated a close relative for over a decade, and informed you that the patient is profoundly ill, deteriorating and close to death, you might enquire as to the effectiveness of the current treatment. If the Doctor replied: 'None at all', you might well ask what he planned to do to remedy the situation. If he then announced that he intended to carry on as he had for the last ten years, you would be forgiven for looking for tell-tale signs – a tick around the corner of the eyes perhaps, or a twitch in the hand. With regards to ailing Planet Earth, new Director David Gee would appear to be inviting a similarly troubled investigation into the course of treatment recommended by Friends of the Earth.

Former Health Officer with the Municipal Boilermakers Union David Gee sees an essential continuity between problems faced in his previous and current roles: 'The technical data behind the ozone layer controversy and global warming is different from that for asbestos, but the nature of the debate is exactly the same. It all turns on how you deal with scientific uncertainty, and whether people and the planet get the benefit of the doubt' (D. Gee, 1990).

The solution to the environmental crisis, then, is essentially a rational one – the amassing of undeniably persuasive, scientifically-corroborated information which will affect the behaviour of politicians, corporations and consumers by tipping the benefit of the doubt in favour of people and planet.

Clearly, scientific accuracy and credibility are crucial: 'We have to be as radical, as scientifically correct and as vociferous on the kinds of solutions which are now needed' (D. Gee, 1990).

Mr Gee recognises that there are inherent difficulties in this approach: ''Politicians hate planning for next week-end let alone the next generation' (D. Gee, 1990).

Nevertheless, because the problem is essentially rational in nature, the steady supply of undeniably 'hard' scientific evidence will win the day, will tip the balance.

This diagnosis is typical of that offered by groups like F.O.E and Greenpeace over the last decade, so it comes as something of a surprise to hear how clearly Mr Gee recognises the extent to which this approach has so far been unsuccessful: 'All F.O.E.'s efforts to get the Government to take energy efficiency seriously ... fell on deaf ears' (D. Gee, 1990). 'It is hard to point to a single fundamental change in policy' (D. Gee, 1990). These quotations are not drawn from disparate sources, but from the same interview, as, I am afraid, is the following: 'We have got this decade left to more or less save the world' (D. Gee, 1990).

Clearly then, according to David Gee, in the decade or so spent supplying the world with rational, scientifically-corroborated information, success has not been forthcoming because too little scientific evidence of sufficient accuracy has been amassed. What we need is more – lots more facts, figures, rational arguments, undeniable evidence – and then things will begin to change.

By way of ironic analogy, I am reminded of the stereotypical consumer: consuming ever more, accumulating ever more material wealth, he remains unhappy. His answer is to consume more, accumulate more, thinking – always – that happiness will come with the next house, the next car. Not once does it occur to him that his answer to happiness is not *quantitatively* insufficient but *qualitatively* mistaken. Happiness is not equatable with material consumption and more consumption means more something, but it does not mean more happiness.

Similarly, the answer to environmental crises does not lie in scientific knowledge alone, because the problem itself not what we know but what we believe. More scientific knowledge changes something, but it does not change the beliefs and the values of Industrial Society. The environmental crisis is a symptom of our values, not our ignorance. Rational argument alone is insufficient, because the values of Industrial Society are characterised precisely by their fundamental irrationality. By way of illustration, I would like to examine one of the examples of the modern belief system that drives Industrial Society and, by consequence, environmental destruction: the idea of 'success'.

The drive for status, for 'success', is one of the great engines of Industrial Society, which believes that happiness, security, feelings of worth rest in being better than others – being more wealthy, powerful, beautiful, famous. In this way, by creating a sort of Ego-fortress, the individual imagines happiness can be constructed and fortified. Material consumption of cars, houses, gadgets, luxuries has this belief as a fundamental motivation. Because it leads to pleasure, and lots of pleasure is equated with happiness, over-consumption is seen as the path to happiness.

Also, because the belief that security can be found in an enlarged Ego is illusory, the persisting and progressive insecurity which results lead individuals to escape into ever more consumption and status-building. 'If he is 'successful', he is valuable; if he is not, he is worthless. The degree of insecurity which results from this orientation can hardly be overestimated' (Erich Fromm – *Man For Himself*).

Scientific knowledge is powerless to change this belief. Instead, it is important for us to understand and tackle its root cause.

According to Erich Fromm, the drive to find security and happiness in status, in what we call 'success', is the result of a regressive attempt to escape feelings of insignificance. Being free from instinctual/habitual behaviour and instead possessing self-awareness, man, unlike other animals, is part of and yet transcends the natural world. Self-awareness is a gift in that it gives man freedom; it is also a curse in that it gives man a feeling of separateness, aloneness. In relation to the world around him, man feels unbearably small, insignificant, transient. The world is infinite – man is finite and fleeting.

Impulses arise to escape these feelings of separateness and insignificance. In a regressive solution, the new-found independence is abandoned, the individual seeking comfort in the dominance of mother, father, a greater cause, an authoritarian state – any thing into which the self can be dissolved. The alternative to removing the self that feels insignificant, is to remove the world that creates the comparison – hence a dominating, possessive, destructive orientation to the world around us. By removing the enormity of the world through destroying, consuming or dominating it, the individual attempts to win a sense of greater worth and value.

Modern society's idea of 'success' is just one such regressive attempt to remove feelings of insignificance. Rooted in the fundamental perception of separateness between man and nature, this orientation is fundamentally hostile to nature. Environmental degradation is a logical consequence of this orientation.

No less unsuccessful than the idea of 'progress' for humanity in general, is the attempt to find happiness through 'success' for individuals in particular. Real security and well-being is achieved only by understanding that, although separate, man is part of a whole. By perceiving the world as separate, the world remains a constant source of anxiety. Our attempts to build expanded fortresses of our Egos serve only to remove us from our reality as part of the whole – and in our isolation, we are ever more anxious, depressed, lonely, confused. Common is the spectacle of the 'successful' who, having come to the logical conclusion of their own delusion, see that they are as insignificant as ever – all their achievements seem meaningless, a charade – and if this is the case, then what is the point to it all?

Because environmentally-destructive consumption is rooted in these types of

'Escape from Freedom', which are themselves profoundly irrational, any attempt to change this behaviour by mere reference to scientific certainty as to its damaging effects – without reference to the sense of alienation and insignificance which is its motivation – is, as the past decade has shown, doomed to failure. Indeed, the Green movement often makes the dangerous and self-defeating assumption that overconsumption is the result of innate greed, selfishness, stupidity – that environmental well-being involves self-sacrifice. In fact, the values of Industrial Society demand the most extraordinary sacrifice of well-being (carefully ignored by all with vested interests in promoting ever-greater consumption) – there is no real conflict of interest.

Only when current ideas of 'success' become incredible to society *en masse* can hard fact be used as a practical guide to the process of changing society – its politics and its economy – into one that promotes well-being in people and in planet. Until then, the task of David Gee – and the Green movement generally – is to set about the erroneous values of society with the ultimate carrot – well-being/reality; and the ultimate stick – global environmental disaster.

DAVID EDWARDS

HEMINGWAY'S LADY AN EDINBURGH CRIMINAL!

If during his lifetime (1899-1961) it had been discovered that one of Ernest Hemingway's closest female associates had committed not one but at least two serious criminal offences in Edinburgh, then it is certain that Scottish newspapers and a goodly portion of the International Press would have trumpeted the facts throughout the world; but this has proved to be the case, as I discovered recently by inspecting the Edinburgh Marriage Certificate (date Thursday 26 January 1917) of Lady Duff Twysden, former Spanish drinking companion of one Ernest Miller Hemingway, world renowned American Novelist.

This was the same lady for whom Hemingway developed an unrequited passion while spending part of 1924 at Spain's Pamplona Bullfighting Festival, and whom he fictionalised as Lady Brett Ashley in 'The Sun Also Rises'. The hard drinking adventuress was portrayed by Ava Gardner in the 1956 film version of the book which also featured Tyrone Power, Errol Flynn and Mel Ferrer.

What then were the Edinburgh crimes of this beautiful but dissipated Anglo-Scottish woman who, despite aristocratic pretensions, could drink and swear as well as any of the males who courted her?

To answer this one must accept that by the time Duff Twysden arrived with her husband-to-be, Royal Navy Lieutenant Roger Twysden, at Edinburgh's Caledonian Hotel (in order to establish residency qualifications prior to marriage), she was well practised in the arts of deception. Not only had she been employed by the British Secret Service in the months preceding her matrimonial journey northwards to 'Auld Reekie', but she had actually met Roger Twysden when the latter was assigned to Naval Intelligence. So the path of romantic falsehood was already well worn by this Yorkshire lass – born plain Dorothy Smurthwaite on May 22nd, daughter of Baines Smurthwaite, a licensed grocer. Her Scots mother, Charlotte Stirling, came from a prosperous Scottish middle class background and had aristocratic pretensions which she had clearly passed on to her wayward daughter. On her Edinburgh Marriage Certificate Duff Twysden's licensed grocer father is magically transformed into a 'Solicitor'. Duff Smurthwaite Twysden had also divorced her first husband, Luttrell Byrom, in 1916. Yet on the matrimonial certificate she wrongly describes herself as a 'widow' thus committing not one but two criminal offences under the Births, Deaths and Marriages (Scotland) Act.

Nevertheless such offences were mere peccadillos to an adventuress who was determined to transform her mother's social climbing fantasies into a daily personal reality by marrying into the minor English landed gentry as represented by the Devon based Twysden's of Churston House. Money and enhanced social position were the catalyst which provoked this beautiful and charming temptress into brazenly flaunting the laws of Scotland, as she and her beau stood in 49 Manor Place, Edinburgh, before the Reverend R. H. Fisher of St. Cuthbert's Parish Church who married them 'according to the forms of the Church of Scotland'. No doubt she displayed to minister and suitor alike that same fatal charm that so impressed Hemingway. Someone who was not fooled by the Smurthwaite charm was Roger Twysden's mother, Jessie. So forcibly did she reject the marital aspirations of her gold digging potential daughter-in-law that she drove the loving couple to elope to Edinburgh. Jessie Twysden's attitude was also partially responsible for the blatant falsehoods of the Edinburgh Marriage Certificate – at least in two respects.

First, the Twysdens were staunch Church of England members who had that same established Church hatred of divorcees that would cost King Edward VIII (Duke of Windsor) his crown in 1936. Secondly, they were gentry who would almost certainly have despised the daughter of a licensed grocer – hence the double falsehoods of 'widow' and 'Solicitor' on the Auld Reekie Marriage Certificate, clear attempts to curry favour with her mother-in-law. Nonetheless Jessie Twysden's forecasts became true. The marriage contracted at 49 Manor Place, Edinburgh ended in England in a welter of alcoholic dissipation and bitchiness. By the time Ernest Hemingway first encountered Duff Twysden in 1924 she was living with her equally dissolute Scottish cousin, Pat Guthrie – a man notorious as a sponger and drunkard portrayed by Errol Flynn under the pseudonym 'Mike Campbell' in the 1950s movie of 'The Sun also Rises'.) Nevertheless, despite being initially infatuated enough with Duff Twysden to make her the first heroine of his novels, Hemingway soon tired of her incessant attempts to cadge money from him.

There was to be no happy ending for this amoral cinderella. By 1933 she had met and married an American painter, Clinton King, with whom she lived until she died aged 43 from tuberculosis on June 27th 1938 at Santa Fe, New Mexico.

Meanwhile, the ghost of Lady Duff Twysden is still beguiling and fooling American writers, particularly those scholars responsible for three large biographies of Hemingway since 1986. All three faithfully repeat the Duff Twysden inspired fiction that Roger Twysden was a Baronet – he was not. English Baronets always append the letters 'Bart' after their surnames – no such appendage appears on the Marriage Certificate that I obtained from Edinburgh's Register House. The same trio also regurgitate the fiction that Roger Twysden was 'A Royal Naval Commander' – the Wedding Certificate clearly states that he was a Lieutenant attached to 'H.M.S. Petard.' Nobody would enjoy more her capacity to put the cat among the academic pigeons from the posthumous distance of fifty-one years than Dorothy Smurthwaite, alias Lady Duff Twysden, alias Brett Ashley.

BRIAN DONALD

HYPERTROPHY

Hyper'troph/y, n. Enlargement (of organ, etc.) due to excessive nutrition. (*The Concise Oxford Dictionary*).

n. (Pathology) A nontumerous increase in size of an organ or part as a result of enlargement, without increase in number, of constituent cells. (*The American Heritage Dictionary of the English Language*)

n. 1. Excessive development of an organ or part; specif.: increase in bulk (as by thickening of muscle fibers without multiplication of parts 2. exaggerated growth or complexity. (*Merriam-Webster's New Collegiate Dictionary*)

* * *

WHEN in the course of human events it became necessary to reName our Great Nation, we deemed it necessary to propose a Radical readdress: HyperTrophy, derived from Pathology.

THIS BEFIT our Great Nation's having come-of-age among great nations, albeit abruptly (in less than a quarter-millenium).

LIKEWISE, having grown beyond our ability to understand ourself, HyperTrophy bespoke our quandary directly lest confusion of intent distract us from our accumulative National Purpose.

FOR OURS is to Increase without Awareness, without increase in the number of, (brain) cells by increase of bulk (as by the thickening of muscle fibers). Growth S'US, hypertrophically, as will now be made evident without explanation beyond naming. Such a name historical necessity demands, and such a name our volatile memory is capable of retaining (with brief refreshment.)

LET US THEN justly relegate our previous, original, obsolete national name to all those nations, collectively, who share our original intent: with malice towards none, with charity for all, without bitterness (amer-ica) at our passing from the scene.

BE THIS DECLARED: WE, who were once AMERICA, stand by our own candor renamed HYPERTROPHY, exaggerated beacon unto the world. Let there be medals and coins struck accordingly. Let our name be spoken loudly (in public places) as well as quietly (in the secret chambers our hearts & our minds.)

DONE this (supply) Day of the Year (supply) of Our reNaming.

BILL COSTLEY

THE KALEVALA

A narrative epic poem of some 22,795 lines which the Finns regard as their national epic.

The poem tells the story of the creation of the world;the adventures of the primordial shaman and magician Vainamöinen and his brother the smith Ilmarinen and of the vitalistic warrior hero Lemminkainen. Pivotal to the action is the rivalry between the Kalevalans (Finns) and the people of Pohjola (the Lapps). There is a prolonged struggle between Louhi the witch queen of Pohjola and the Kalevalans for possession of the 'sampo', a magic object which generates unlimited wealth.There are also several sub-plots which deal with Lemminkainen's exploits and the lifelong quest for revenge by the doomed Kullervo.

The status of The Kalevala as one of the unquestionable classics of world literature is barely recognised in the English-speaking world, perhaps due to the geo-graphical remoteness of Finland and the difficulties presented by its culture and by the Finnish language, a Uralian tongue related only to Magyar, Estonian, Lappish and some minority Siberian languages. Its influence on Finnish culture and even political life has been incalculable; notably it inspired some of the major works of Sibelius which have provided the few points of access to the epic for the English-speaking world.

Orally transmitted folk poetry,often chanted or sung to the accompaniment of a 'kantele', an instrument resembling a zither, was a tradition possibly dating as far back as the migration of the Finns and Estonians from central Asia to the Baltic region somewhere between the 1st and 5th centuries A.D. However, literature in Finnish barely existed before 1835. The country was ruled by Sweden from 1155 to 1809, when it was ceded to Russia; Swedish was the language of administration and culture.

Oral folk poetry survived largely in Karelia, the most eastern part of Finland, though in pagan times it was probably predominant in Häme in the central and southern part of the country. A Finnish doctor named Elias Lönnrot (1802-1884) travelled extensively in Karelia and collected a huge body of folk poetry.From this he constructed a coherent epic with the model of Homer in mind.

The number of lines in The Kalevala actually composed by Lönnrot was very small, but he selected and fashioned his material consciously and carefully. As a compendium of authentic folk poetry and folklore The Kalevala is therefore only partially reliable, a fact too often ignored. It represents, rather, the fusion of a genuine, pagan consciousness and a sophisticated 19th century mind.

In the 19th century, the epic became a focal point for cultural pride and the awakening Finnish nationalist movement which was to lead to independence from Russia. More important for our own time are artistic and philosophical elements such as the contrast between the doomed, obsessive, authoritarian Kullervo and the instinctive, life-enhancing Lemminkainen – a symbolic clash between pessimistic rationalism and 'history' on the one hand and natural vitality on the other.

W. F. Kirby's 1907 translation preserves the original trochaic, alliterative verse form but is too often archaic and clumsy. F. P. Magoun's prose version is accurate but does not do justice to the poem's literary greatness. The most recent English translation, by Keith Bosley (Oxford, 1989), avoids the faults of both Kirby's and Magoun's versions and is impressive for its sensitivity, gusto and stylistic daring.

ANTHONY JAMES

Bibliography

The Kalavala. Translated by W. F. Kirby (Athlone Press.)

The Kalavala. Translated by F. P. Magoun (Harvard University Press.)

Finnish Folk Poetry Epic. An anthology in Finnish and English. Edited and translated by Matti Kuusi / Keith Bosley / Michael Branch (Finnish Literature Society 1977).

LAMENNAIS & LES PAROLES D'UN CROYANT

Lamennais's view, put simply, was that religious understanding and the teaching of Christ must lead to a way of living that reflects those truths. The responsibility of the (Roman Catholic) Church was to defend religious freedom and to uphold all those who sought to live according to Christ's teaching.

When the newspaper that Lamennais edited came under attack from the French Church hierarchy, he and his co-editors appealed direct to Rome. That newspaper, *l'Avenir* (The Future), had as its slogan: 'For God and Liberty'. It reported all forms of religious persecution, both in France and abroad, and actively campaigned on behalf of those struggling for religious freedom. In particular, a cause dear to the readers of *l'Avenir* was the fate of the Polish people: they had risen against the Tsar in 1830, to be savagely repressed by Russian troops a year later, and their goal had been not only political but religious freedom, the right to choose Catholic rather than Russian Orthodox imposed religious authority.

The Pope's dilemma, in receiving Lamennais' appeal, was that if he agreed with Lamennais, he would be attacked by all the autocratic governments of Europe for supporting rebellion, yet if he disagreed with Lamennais, he would be undermining his own moral position. What Lamennais had always declared was that the Pope should be appealed to as the defender of Christianity over and above any national government or even national Church.

In the event, either from personal conviction or as a consequence of political pressure, Pope Gregory XVI condemned Lamennais and his followers in an encyclical issued in 1832. *L'Avenir* was to close and the editors were to sign a complete submission. Given Lamennais' claim that religious authority ought to lie with the Pope, he could hardly do other than sign a declaration of submission and, in any case, his office as a priest required him so to do. But it was a bitter blow.

Following his return from Rome, Lamennais withdrew to his native Brittany and there composed the remarkable book *Les Paroles d'un Croyant* (The Words of a Believer). The book appeared in 1834 and was an immediate success, running into some hundred editions. The printers themselves left their presses to run into the streets and recite parts of the text, crowds gathered in Paris parks to hear students read from the book and people queued outside reading rooms so that they could read the book at so much an hour. The book was praised and defended by the weak and the poor everywhere and just as fiercely condemned by the powerful and the rich.

The book is composed of 42 chapters and structured in the same way as the Bible with verses to each chapter. Like the Bible, it contains prophecy and apocalyptic visions, pastoral interludes, attacks on the rich and powerful much in the way of Hosea or Amos, moral teachings in parables and words of comfort to the distressed. The slogans of the Revolution are here re-presented as religious, not just political, truths. Equality, Lamennais states, derives from our common father who is God; Liberty is a right we must demand since both master and slave contradict the religious principle of Equality; and Brotherhood is a duty that we owe to others, to love one another as God loves each one of us. The whole book is firmly rooted in Christian theology.

What also comes through powerfully is Lamennais' identification with the common people (XXVII) and an unrelenting attack on all those wielding power against them, whether that power be exercised in the name of politics or religion (XIX). In particular, chapter XXXIII is a wide ranging attack on all the most repressive governments of Europe. He attacks capitalism (VIII: see below) and makes a powerful attack on militarism (XXXV) although he also identifies with what today would be called liberation struggles (XXXVI).

For Lamennais, the book marked his break with the Church, though he was never excommunicated and for a time continued to attend mass. Not least among the reasons for the hostility of the Church hierarchy was the famous passage in chapter XXXIII, in which the Pope is shown signing a pact with Tsar Nicholas I to whom Gregory XVI had ordered the Polish bishops to show allegiance following the capitulation of Warsaw. But the whole tone of the book, identifying itself with those who were struggling for independence, was enough to anger powerful interests. Lamennais was forced to resign his office as Superior of the Congregation of St. Peter (later itself dissolved), his friends abandoned him, and he had to take to political journalism for a living.

Lamennais continued to prepare scholarly and philosophical works, but it was for his political writing that he became more popularly known. In particular, *Le Pays et le Gouvernement* (The Country and the Government) earned him a prison sentence of 12 months in 1841. Lamennais played a part in the political activity that led to the revolution of 1848 and was elected deputy to the new National Assembly. Following the *coup d'état* of 1851 which brought Louis Napoleon to power, Lamennais withdrew from political life.

Lamennais died in 1854 at the age of 72. At his own request, he was buried in an unmarked grave at Père-Lachaise in Paris.

Further Reading:
Gibson, The Hon. W. *The Abbé de Lammennais and the Liberal Catholic movement in France*, London, 1896
Vidler, A .R. *Prophecy and Papacy*, London, 1954
Roe, W .G. *Lamennais and England*, Oxford, 1966

CHRIS WEEKS

Here follows Ch 8 of *Les Paroles*, translated by Chris Weeks:

VIII

In the beginning, man did not need to work in order to live: the earth itself furnished all his needs.

But man committed evil: and in as much as man turned against God, so did the earth turn against him.

What happened to him was that which happens to a child who turns against his father; the father withdraws his love and leaves him to his own devices; and the house servants refuse to serve him, and he goes forth seeking his livelihood hither and thither, and eating the bread which he has earned by the sweat of his brow.

Since that time then, God has condemned all men to work, and all have their labour, either physical or mental; but those who say: I shall not work, they are the most wretched.

For, as worms consume a corpse, so vices consume them, and if not vices then boredom.

And when God willed that man should work, he hid treasure in that work, because he is a father, and a father's love does not die.

And he who makes good use of that treasure, and does not waste it stupidly, there comes to him a time of rest, and he comes to a time like unto the life of men at the beginning of time.

And, furthermore, God gave them a rule: Help one another, for there are among you the strongest and the weakest, the lame and the able-bodied; yet nevertheless all ought to have life.

And if you conduct yourselves in this

manner, all will have life, for I shall reward the pity that you have shown your brothers, and I shall render your sweat fertile.

And that which God promised has become true for all time, and never has he who helps his brother lacked bread.

Now, there was once an evil man, cursed by heaven. And this man was strong, and he hated work; so that he said unto himself: What should I do? If I do not work, I shall die, but work is intolerable to me.

And so, a hellish thought came into his heart. He went forth at night time, and seized some of his brethren while they slept, and set them in chains.

For, he said, I shall force them, with canes and whip, to work for me, and I shall eat of the fruit of their toil.

And he did, even as he had thought, and others seeing it did likewise, and there were no more brethren, but there were masters and there were slaves.

This was a day of mourning over all the earth.

A long time afterwards, there was another man, even more wicked than the first and more cursed by heaven.

Seeing that humankind had multiplied throughout, and that their multitude was without number, he said to himself:

I could well put some in chains perhaps, and force them to work for me; but they would have to be fed, and that would diminish my profit. Let us do better; rather that they should work for nothing! They will die, it is true, but since their number is great, I shall amass riches before their number has greatly decreased, and there will always remain enough of it.

Whereupon all this multitude did live by that which they received in exchange for their toil.

Having thus spoken in this way, he addressed himself specially to some and said to them: You work for six hours, and you are given a coin for your work.

Work for twelve hours, and you will be given two coins, and you will live better, you, your wives and your children.

And they believed him.

And following this, he said to them:

You only work half the days of the year: work all the days of the year, and your income will be doubled.

And they believed him again.

Now, it came to pass that the amount of work had become greater by half, without the need for work becoming greater, so that half of those who had lived by their labour formerly did not find any who would employ them.

And so, the evil man, whom they had believed, said to them: I shall give work to all, on condition that you work for just as many hours but I pay you half of what I now pay you; for I would like to do good unto you, but I do not wish to be ruined.

And, since they were hungry, they, their wives and their children, they accepted the evil man's proposal, and they blessed him, for, they said, he has given us life.

And, continuing to cheat them in this way, the evil man always added more to their work, and always further reduced their wages.

And they died, lacking the necessities of life, and others pressed forward to take their place since poverty had become so great in that land that whole families sold themselves for a morsel of bread.

And the evil man who had cheated his brothers amassed more riches than the evil man who had put them in chains.

The name of this last is Tyrant, the other has no name except in hell.

MANNERHEIM, CARL GUSTAF EMIL, (1867-1951)

A Finnish military and political leader who was not only a vitally important figure in the history of Finland, but also a statesman whose long and eventful life illustrates the collision of the world of the 19th century with the new forces of the 20th century. In a sense, Mannerheim's life dramatises many of the conflicts and ambiguities of modern European history.

His family was aristocratic and cultured; the Mannerheims were Finno-Swedes – an ethnic group which has always possessed a hybrid culture as distinctive as that of the French-Canadians. Like many privileged circles in the mid-19th century, Mannerheim's family had absorbed the optimistic liberalism which followed the revolutions of 1848. 'I was born in a period when the liberal political ideas spread their enlightenment on mankind,' he later wrote. He never abandoned his commitment to the idea of liberty and equality before the law, and his later actions can only be understood in terms of this preoccupation, from which his strengths and deficiencies stemmed.

In the late 19th century ,Finland was a semi-independent possession of Tsarist Russia, a vast empire with a ruling class that was deeply hostile to Finland's western affinities. When Mannerheim's family became impoverished and he had to earn his living as a young man, he joined the Imperial Russian army, a career which suited his lifelong need for demanding activity, travel and adventure as well as indulging his interest in horses. He was a highly successful officer who served in the Russian-Japanese war of 1905 and in the First World War; he also led a scientific expedition into remote areas of Asia.

Finland declared its independence on December 6th 1917 and consistent with his policy regarding the nationalities of the former empire, Lenin recognised its sovereignty. However, it was Lenin's design that the Russian revolution would lead to revolutions throughout Europe. and the Bolsheviks encouraged their supporters in Finland to seize power.

Mannerheim had by now returned to Finland and set about creating a Finnish army. He was no doubt hostile to the idea of working class political domination, but the Bolsheviks also deeply offended his notions of individual liberty and legality.

He perceived that Finland was in danger of becoming a nominally independent colony of the Bolsheviks, as it had once been a colony of the Tsar. When in 1918 the Finnish Red Guard, formed from the most left-wing elements of the Social Democratic party and detachments of Russian soldiers who supported Lenin, seized power in Helsinki, Mannerheim's army defeated them in a three month civil war. However, he played no part in the reactionary bloodbath which followed

and also opposed the direct involvement of German troops.

Mannerheim was defeated in the new republic's first presidential election in 1919. Shortly before this election and again between 1930 and 1932, when a fascist movement arose briefly in Finland, he had the clear opportunity of making himself military dictator of Finland, but declined to do so.

During the short, desperately fought Winter War of 1939-1940 against the Soviet Union and in the Continuation War of 1941-1944, he led the Finns with great energy and skill, but also consistently recommended diplomacy and tact in dealing with Moscow, in place of the peremptory briskness characteristic of Finnish politicians. During the Continuation War, Finland fought alongside Nazi Germany. Mannerheim treated Hitler and the Nazi leadership with a mixture of aristocratic politeness and aloof disdain and his influence was decisive in preserving Finland's independence as a liberal democracy. He became president from 1944 to 1946, concluding a peace agree-ment with Moscow. In the initial post war period, Stalin obviously regarded Mannerheim as a more reliable Finnish leader than politicians of either the Right or Left.

Mannerheim has been portrayed by left-wing circles as a fascist or fascist sympathiser. The entry in *The Great Soviet Encyclopaedia* and Trotsky's writings on Finland in the collection *In Defence of Marxism* both clearly state this. However, he openly declared his distaste for German and Italian fascism in the 1930's and exerted himself to protect Jews to whom Finland had given refuge from the Nazis during the War. Similarly, he made efforts to bring about national reconciliation after the Finnish civil war. He was in fact an old-fashioned 19th century liberal in a position of immense power, confronted by the new totalitarian systems of the 20th century.

ANTHONY JAMES

OEDIPUS
(Translation from Cavafy, an early uncollected poem.)

The Sphinx is fallen upon him,

teeth and talons exposed,
and with all the ferocity of life.
Oedipus fell at her first onslaught;
her first appearance terrified him –
such a form, such speech,
he had never imagined until then.
But for all that the monster's two feet
rested on Oedipus's breast,
he soon got used to it – and now,
he's not afraid at all, because he has
the answer ready, and will win.
But he doesn't rejoice at this victory.
His gaze full of melancholy,
he looks, not at the Sphinx, but
     further:
the narrow road that leads to Thebes,
and will end at Colonnus.
And his soul foresees clearly
that there the Sphinx will speak again:
more difficult, greater enigmas,
that have no answer.

SIMON DARRAGH

PRESUMED INNOCENT

That *Presumed Innocent* received such
positive critical reviews is indicative both
of the popular (male) appeal of its insidi-
ous subplot and of the fact that critics
may be good on film history and genre
analysis, but appalling when it comes to
spotting reactionary garbage.

Faithfully adapted from Scott Thur-
low's best selling novel, *Presumed Innocent* has been acclaimed a classic of the
Court Room genre and politically astute
in its revelations of the corruption which
surrounds the U.S. judicial hierarchy and
D.A. elections.

The plot is presented as a straightforward *Who dunnit?* Rusty Saich, deputy
prosecuting attorney, is called upon to
investigate the brutal rape and murder of
his colleague and former lover, Carolyn
Polhemus. The evidence begins to point
in his direction and he finds himself on
trial for her murder.

The dead woman's character and
motivations are central to the film:
through flashbacks, we see her seduce
Rusty and try to manipulate him so as to
improve her career prospects. She is talented and intelligent, yet she chooses to
advance her status through predatory
female sexuality, bribery and corruption.

In contrast to Carolyn stands Rusty's
wife, Barbara. Though hurt when she
discovers Rusty's affair with Carolyn,
Barbara has stuck by him and is completely
loyal when he is accused of murder.
Throughout the trial scenes this is visually
reinforced by reassuring close-ups of Rusty
in the dock, with his wife in frame behind
him.

The way in which Carolyn was murdered is suggestive: she was tied up in such
a way that she was strangled to death as
she was being raped. The women jurors
are particularly horrified by the photographs of the murder. Surely only a psy-
chotic man could have done this? The
evidence found at the scene – a tumbler
with his finger prints on it, his semen in
her vagina – points to Rusty. However, he
is acquitted, as a result of misplaced evidence and the judge's dodgy past. While
the viewer still has doubts about Rusty's
innocence, the male characters in the film
don't really seem to care one way or the
other. Rusty's detective buddy even reveals that he stole the tumbler, not because
he believed in Rusty's innocence, but out
of loyalty and because Carolyn was no
good: 'She deserved to die.'

As we are led towards the conclusion,
the film reveals its roots in the reactionary
preoccupations of the late 1980s: AIDS-
led prescriptive morality and the fear of
successful women. Carolyn is successful
and ambitious. It is acknowledged that
she is a good lawyer, but in order to
emphasise her as 'other', the field of pros-
ecution she prefers most is the area of
sexual abuse. Her compassion leads her
to specialise in an area that most ambitious lawyers avoid. This compassion
defines her as 'other', as a woman, yet it
is strangely at odds with her other defining characteristic, the use of her sexuality
to manipulate men and achieve personal
goals.

In *Misogynies* (Faber, 1989), Joan
Smith observes that in the novel 'women's
power is always achieved illegitimately
and at the expense of men, and sometimes
at the expense of other women... female
intrusion into public life – into male areas
of life – inevitably brings with it the risk
that violence will ensue.' The fact that

Carolyn was engaged in prosecuting sex offenders made her prone to revenge attacks: ironically, however, her death is not the result of her work, but of her intrusion on the male world in which she operated as a temptress, threatening other women and the security of the family. The revelation that Barbara (driven by jealousy) is the murderer does not alter the fact that, as Smith states, it is Carolyn who is 'the true culprit, the real cause of the crime'. Resolving the conflicts which Carolyn introduced into the status quo, Barbara's crime of murder goes unpunished by the law, while Rusty's crime of adultery again throws the blame onto the dead Carolyn. Perhaps the most galling aspect of this film is the use of another woman to resolve the conflict of Carolyn's challenge to male power and, by thus masking the real issue, to give credence to the notion that women perpetuate their own oppression.

LISA HONAN

REFUSAL OF LEAVE TO LAND REPORT (REMARKS)

Mr VLIET was detained in the approved detention quarters in the Queen's Building from 1230 hours until 1700 hours. He had previously remained in the Arrivals Hall.

Mr VLIET is the leader of an American 'pop group' known as Captain Beefheart's Magic Band, which specialises in so-called psychedelic music and is currently very popular with a certain section of the population of the West Coast of the United States. The group arrived together and presented a very strange appearance, being attired in clothing ranging from 'jeans' to purple trousers, with shirts of various hues, and wearing headgear varying from conical witches' hats to a brilliant yellow safety helmet of the type worn by construction engineers. Like some of his friends, Mr VLIET sported a bushy beard. The other members of the group whose refusal of leave to land is reported separately, are:

FRENCH, John Stephen born 29.9.48 American

HANDLEY, Gerald Wayne born 9.2.46 American

SNOUFFER, Alexis Clair born 14.9.41 American

COTTON, Jeffrey Ralph born 31.5.40 American

Officers on the control were given ample opportunity to form an initial assessment of the group, as they took fully ten minutes to complete the relatively simple operation of filling in their landing cards. When they eventually approached the desks, it proved somewhat difficult to interview them, as they appeared to think on a completely different mental plane and found it difficult to grasp the rudiments of a passport control. However, it was eventually established that they had gone to Hanover from the United States to attend a musical convention and that they were now en route to a similar festival in Nice. All five members of the group possessed tickets from London to Nice and on to Los Angeles and they said that they merely wished to spend up to a week in this country on the way to France. None of them appeared very certain what the purpose of the visit to this country was, some saying that it was purely for a rest and others saying that they were to meet representatives of the Press. However, all of them denied emphatically that they had any intention of taking any form of employment during their stay. Examination of the funds carried by the group showed that they had very little money, Mr VLIET having £2.10.0; and 20 marks (£2).

At this stage, a gentleman dressed in the American style, with long unkempt hair and with a cigarette dangling from his lower lip, approached the control and introduced himself as Mr Peter Alexander Edwin MEADEN, born 11.11.41, British and described in his passport as an Artistes Manager. Mr MEADEN said that he represented New Wave Records Ltd, 17-19 Stratford Place, LONDON, W.1., which firm was sponsoring the group's visit to the United Kingdom, in conjunction with the group's American recording company, Kama Sutra Buddha Records Ltd., New York. He offered to give any guarantees that might be required to facilitate the group's entry into the country but when asked to establish his authority to do so, he was unable to prove his connection with these companies beyond producing a press handout and some blank headed notepaper. Mr MEADEN denied vehemently that the group would be taking any form of work during their stay here and said that he had only brought them over for press appearances.

At this stage, all five members of the group were escorted to the baggage hall, where their luggage was examined by H. M. Customs. However, despite the fact that one member of the group had a large number of patent medicines in his case, nothing of interest was found. A search of the group's instruments and their cases was also negative.

On return to the Arrivals Hall, I was informed by an officer of the Special Branch that Mr MEADEN was known to have convictions for illegal possession of a bren gun, taking and driving away a motor vehicle and selling intoxicating liquor without a licence. In view of this, it was felt that any assurances given by the gentleman would have to be treated with considerable reservations.

It was strongly suspected that the group were going to take engagements in this country and reference to the New Musical Express showed that they were billed to appear at two establishments the next weekend, namely the Middle Earth Club and the SpekeEasy Club, both in the West End of London. These clubs were telephoned and confirmed that the group would be playing on stage as a professional engagement. Reference to the Ministry of Labour showed that Mr MEADEN had applied for Ministry of Labour Permits for the Middle Earth Club engagement but that none had been issued, as he had claimed that the group were only to meet the Press at the club and would not be playing – denied by the club who were expecting a full show. Faced with this Mr MEADEN at first protested his innocence but finally both he and the group admitted that the engagements had been arranged. Mr MEADEN then pleaded for clemency on the grounds of his own stupidity, a plea which was rejected.

The case was referred to the Chief Immigration Officer, Mr Armstrong, who directed that the group be refused leave to land on the grounds that they had come to this country to take unauthorised employment and with insufficient funds. They were informed that they were at liberty so contact whomsoever they wished and spent some time on the telephone before going to the Detention Suite, where they were given a meal.

As it seemed that the group were to a considerable extent the innocence in what was by now a very tangled web woven largely by Mr MEADEN, it was decided to make some effort on their behalf beyond the call of duty. To this end, the Chief Immigration Officer, Mr R.A. Mac-Dowall, spent some four hours on the telephone liaising with the Home Office, the Ministry of Labour, Pye Records and Equity. Pye came into the picture because the President of Kama Sutra Records, Mr Artie RIPP, an American, was with the company negotiating some form of take-over bid by Pye for his company. Mr MacDowall spoke with Mr Ripp and with Mr WISE of Pye and advised them that they should contact the Ministry of Labour and Equity and apply for permits. Should they be issued, then the position would be reconsidered in a favourable light.

Mr Noreiko, Chief Immigration Officer, Headquarters, was informed of the case, lest there should be any representations. These soon materialised, from Mr MEADEN'S solicitor, who asked that the group be admitted for a visit. This proposal was rejected.

Later in the afternoon, H. M. Assistant Chief Inspector, Mr T.W.E. Roche telephoned for details of the case, as the Press Officer had approached him for information.

Despite all their efforts, which were considerable, Mr Ripp and Mr Wise were unable to secure the issue of Ministry of Labour Permits and the group were therefore returned to Hanover as directed.

Mr MEADEN, on whose shoulders the blame for the whole incident must rest, was told by Mr Ripp that his association with Kama Sutra ceased forthwith and he was a dejected man as he finally departed, muttering under his breath. Landing Card attached. An extra copy of this report is attached for the Ministry of Labour.

texte trouvée
dated 24th January, 1968

SAX ROHMER

Pseudonym of Arthur Ward (15 February 1883 – 1 June 1959), author of over forty novels and dozens of short stories, songs, &c. In his youth he worked as a bank clerk. His first short stories were accepted for publication in 1903. He married Rose Elizabeth Knox, 14 January 1909, thereby becoming brother-in-law of Teddy Knox, the *Crazy Gang* partner of Jimmy Nervo. In his early writing career he concentrated on popular songs (for George Robey and others), advertising copy and short stories. He ghosted the autobiography of Harry Relph (the comedian 'Little Tich'). In 1913 he wrote *The Mystery of Doctor Fu Manchu*, the first of a long and phenomenally successful series of fictions. He dabbled briefly after the war in the manufacture of the perfume *Honan*, employing Chinese immigrant labour in Limehouse. Film rights and continuing public demand for his fiction brought him great wealth between the wars. Both Paramount and MGM made films of his *Fu Manchu* novels: MGM received formal protests from Chinese diplomats, to Rohmer's disbelief. He visited America, where he befriended Houdini, with whom he shared an interest in the occult, but remained based in England until after World War 2 when, his money running out, he emigrated. In the United States he began again to build up his fortune, falling back on the popular success of the *Fu Manchu* series, which concluded with *Emperor Fu Manchu*. He died of Asiatic 'flu in 1959.

Afficianados cite works of horror such as *The Brood of the Witch Queen* and *Grey Face* as among his finest work, but Rohmer's reputation nowadays rests almost entirely on his *Fu Manchu* novels. These have retained their appeal while most of his other works (such as the unreadable *Dope* [1919] and the twaddley

The Dream Detective stories) have been consigned to critical oblivion. The *Fu Manchu* stories all follow the same basic pattern: the Chines master criminal' obscure plot to seize control of the world is thwarted by the efforts of Sir Denis Nayland Smith and a gallery of insipid heroes. One is struck most by the sheer degree of absurdity, the flimsiness of plot, and the one-dimensional quality of the characters who people these severely polite mysteries. Exasperation threatens the most stubborn reader. But: 'the spirit of the thing was beginning to get me. Truly this was a desperate adventure... for the stakes were life or death!' (*Daughter of Fu Manchu*).

Never can life have been so thoroughly predictable or death so welcome a relief as in the world of Sax Rohmer. The pursuit of the criminal genius continues at breakneck speed, but to no effect: he invariably escapes at the moment of crisis to fight another day. Quite what Fu Manchu's motives are, and why his master-plan is conducted in the most ineffectively labyrinthine manner imaginable, is uncertain. All we get is rare glimpses of the point of it all:

"'Who is he, sir, exactly, this Dr. Fu-Manchu?'

"I have only the vaguest idea, Inspector; but he is no ordinary criminal. He is the greatest genius which the powers of evil have put on earth for centuries. He has the backing of a political group whose wealth is enormous and his mission in Europe is to *pave the way!* Do you follow me?"'

Not quite. But this is about as much information as we ever get. This idea of pure, sinister threat is the Hitchcockian 'McGuffin' on which Rohmer hangs his thrills. Rohmer is not only cryptic, he is repetitive: any or all of the *Fu Manchu* novels could have their chapters muddled up without any sense of impropriety. Some repeat lengthy passages, or feature parallel descriptions of events: things happen in the narrative, then later one character explains them again to those who were not present when they first happened. The sense of *deja vu* this produces in the inattentive reader may become disorienting. The figure of *Fu Manchu* is itself a kind of repetition, an echo of Poe's 'Man of the Crowd', De Quincey's urban menace of 'The Avenger' and 'Murder as a Fine Art (Postscript)', and Conan Doyle's Moriarty. Rohmer places himself firmly in this tradition – mimicking De Quincey's Radcliffe Highway of impenetrable Oriental faces in his descriptions of Limehouse, aping Moriarty's descent into a waterfall (*President Fu Manchu*) – but what is perhaps distinctly modern about him is the heightened sense of vertiginous paranoia which informs his work ('I believe a sense of being followed is a recognized nervous disorder; but it was one I had never experienced without finding it to be based on fact' [*Daughter of Fu Manchu*]). As the cliché goes, 'Just because you're paranoid doesn't mean they're not out to get you'. Nothing happens, repeatedly: the fictions are fundamentally hollow and only once, in *Bride of Fu Manchu* (the best of the series), is the existential emptiness confronted: what all the characters are trying to do is overcome death, overcome a sense of generalised emptiness.

In counterpoint to the background of obscure international conspiracy, the violence in the novels takes place chiefly on a personal and domestic level: people do not sit in chairs, they hurl themselves into them; they do not speak, they 'rap' and 'snap'. The settings are often exotic, but one gets the barest sense of their features: a few hillsides, some menacing orientals or negroes – but never anything as menacing as the banal interiors of the hero's rooms in a quintessentially Western Hotel.

The real exotic element in the novels is provided by the female characters. The world of men – of political action, adventure, violent death and so forth – is the realm of good and evil, of moral dilemma. Rohmer's women stand out against this, in a limbo that is sometimes immoral, more often amoral – in a world of potentiality which makes the ludicrous chase after Fu Manchu seem dull. They add the spice to life, and if Nayland Smith's smug remark that 'women are very much alike – very much alike from Charing Cross to

Pagoda Road' (*The Devil Doctor*) comically reveals the severity of his narrowmindedness, it also emphasises Rohmer's contention that women are a universal glue who, criminal conspiracy or no criminal conspiracy (who cares?), provide the chase with its real thrills.

M. O'C

A TRAIL OF MUCUS

Plump breasts of stalactite: spring
    grottos sprouting goose quills.
Jaggy crags make dog's teeth with the
    zig-zag pool.
I laugh at myself, 'curled in the bosom'
    and with horns pulled in,
then wind back up the misty steps, just
    like a snail.

Tu Mu

Prompted by the molluscan imagery of this T'ang dynasty poet, one may turn one's thoughts from the clear calciferous colostrum of the stalactites to a particular form of artificial cream. According to 'The Bulwark' for May 1907 land snails were much used in England then for the manufacture of cream. Indeed, a retired milkman is mentioned as pronouncing it the most successful imitation known. In this matter one may be more a sceptic than an eager experimenter for, unless it were just a matter of adding a little slime to milk, there could be less labour in milking a cow than in creaming the necessary dozens of snails. Be that as it may, garden snails were at one time much eaten in Britain. In recent years, moreover, a number of snail farms have been started, in response to the over-collection of 'escargots' (Roman snails) on the Continent. (Pliny recorded the introduction of experimental 'cochlearia' in Tarquinium in 50 BC. Some say that it was the Romans that introduced Roman snails to England, but the shells have been found in archaeological sites that predate the Roman invasion.)

Aside from being relished as food, snails have also been used to treat a variety of ailments, as also have slugs. Notable amongst these diseases is pulmonary tuberculosis. According to the Doctrine of Signatures, remedies should be sought amongst those things that resemble either some symptom of the disease or the afflicted organ itself and there is an obvious resemblance between the slime of snails and slugs and pulmonary mucus. Slugs swallowed alive were once regarded as an excellent specific for consumption and even in this century a poultice of slugs placed on the chest was regarded as beneficial for respiratory complaints. Beneath the saddle-like area on the back of a slug one may find, if one cares to dissect, a group of small, white, calcareous granules. These were once considered useful in the treatment of dysentery and, according to Pliny, of bad teeth also. In many parts of England there was a belief, even in this century, that slugs could be used to remove warts: rub well with the slug; impale the slug on a thorn; as the slug dries and withers, so does the wart. (I have not tried this, but I have observed the stripping of paint by slime left by mating slugs. This, however, was the result of the latter's contraction on drying and not of chemical action or magic.) In Yorkshire, snails used to provided a greenish salve for corns, and in the 1880s plasters, sold at a penny each in London, were made from papers over which garden snails had crawled. Martin Lister recorded further uses for snails in 1678. He noted that the fluid obtained by pricking them (slime, with perhaps some admixture of other fluids) was used in bleaching wax for artistic purposes. Mixed with the white of egg, it was also used for making a firm cement.

The slugs and snails themselves put their mucus to even more varied uses. (I call it mucus now as this seems to be a respectable word amongst zoologists, and more specific.) Mucus is produced by special cells that are distributed generally over the exposed body surface, but it is also secreted by a gland that opens onto the animal's underside. The mucus aids in crawling and it helps to protect the skin. It comes in various forms and has various other functions. Thus, some slugs and snails secrete a white, milky mucus in response to irritation, but otherwise produce a clear mucus; the corresponding mucus elicited by prodding a garden snail is yellow. More remarkable are the long strings of mucus at the end of which some slugs mate. This they do while hanging in the air from trees, the hermaphrodite couple entwined in a lovers' knot.

Snails avoid desiccation in dry weather by retiring into their shells. Many of them use then their mucus to seal themselves to rocks and other solid surfaces. Others cover over the mouths of their shells with one or more curtains of dried mucus. Thus protected against desiccation and intruders, the snails may remain dormant for many years if need be. (There is an account of snails waking up after fifteen years of sleep, but a more acceptable maximum is nearer half that.) The Roman snail secretes such mucus curtains when it becomes dormant in summer, but when it prepares for hibernation it lays down a thick 'pot lid' of chalky material that is formed from a different mucus.

Whether for such pot lids, for egg shells, or for their own shells, snails require calcium. They flourish best, therefore, where there is chalk or limestone. Some calcium is taken in with the food, but snails are also able to absorb it through the soles of their feet. Indeed, I have often observed pet snails with their feet outspread on lumps of chalk. It is not clear whether the mucus has a role in dissolving the material. In a few areas where there are cliffs of carboniferous limestone this is almost honeycombed with tunnels made by garden snails. The snails shelter in these tiny caves, at least during winter, and, by eroding just a little of the rock, enlarge them gradually over the years, or, for all I know, over centuries. The caves that Tu Mu visited were clearly in limestone, as attested by the presence of stalactites, so that there would probably have been real snails nearby to inspire him.

R. F. BURTON

EDINBURGH UNIVERSITY PRESS
22 George Square, Edinburgh EH8 9LF

THE
FABULOUS MATTER OF FACT
The Poetics of
Neil M Gunn

Richard Price

July 1991 344pp 216x138mm cased 0 7486 0259 3 £22.50

The Fabulous Matter of Fact is a comprehensive study of all Gunn's extant novels (including an early unpublished novel), and a detailed account of the literary context Gunn saw himself working within. Best remembered for his evocative accounts of Highland life in *The Silver Darlings, Morning Tide* and *Highland River*, Neil Gunn was also recognised by his contemporaries Hugh MacDiarmid and TS Eliot as an important and interesting writer. Price describes Gunn's early literary relationship with the Celtic Twilight writers of the late 19th century, arguing that he was much more literarily conscious than has been generally believed.

Including useful plot summaries and a radical re-reading of the novels from the mid-1940s onwards, this is the most wide-ranging and approachable guide to the work of Neil M Gunn currently available.

Richard Price is an Information Officer at the British Library, London, co-founder and editor of the literary magazine, *Gairfish*, and editor of *Verse*.

Carlos Alvarez was born in Spain in 1933. His work was suppressed under Franco. More biographical details on p.18.

Malcolm Green was born in Essex in 1952 and now lives in Heidelberg. His translations of German Expressionist stories, *The Golden Bomb*, will be published by Polygon in spring 1992.

Robert Alan Jamieson is a writer from Shetland. His novel *A Day at the Office* will be published this summer.

David Johnston teaches Spanish at Queen's University, Belfast. Recent translations include Lorca's *Blood Wedding* and *Yerma*, and Lope de Vega's *The Knight from Olmedo*.

Anne Mullen was born in Glasgow in 1964. She is currently a research student at St Anne's College Oxford, working on contemporary Sicilian literature.

David Mackenzie is from Easter Ross and now lives in London. His first novel, *The Truth of Stone* was published by Mainstream in spring 1991.

Frans Masereel was one of the great printmaker-communicators of this century. His novels without words, first published in the thirties, have recently been republished by Redstone Press.

Cildo Meireles was born in Rio de Janeiro in 1948. He has been exhibiting his work internationally since 1970.

Bridget Penney was born in Edinburgh in 1964 and lives in London. She is author of *Honeymoon with death and other stories*, published by Polygon in 1991.

Charles Stephens lives in Cambridge. His first book of essays *Shakespeare's Island* will be published in 1992.

Lorna J. Waite is a working-class writer from Kilbirnie Ayrshire. She now lives in Muirhouse, Edinburgh.